Creative Relaxation

Creative

TURNING YOUR STRESS

Dr. Deborah Bright

Relaxation

INTO POSITIVE ENERGY

New York and London
Harcourt Brace Jovanovich

Requests for permission to make copies
of any part of the work should be mailed to:
Permissions, Harcourt Brace Jovanovich, Inc.
757 Third Avenue, New York, N.Y. 10017

Printed in the United States of America

LIBRARY OF CONGRESS CATALOGING IN PUBLICATION DATA
Bright, Deborah.
Creative relaxation.
1. Stress (Psychology)   2. Relaxation.   I. Title
BF575.S75B74   158'.1   79-1815
ISBN 0-15-122802-7

First edition
B   C   D   E

Thanks to my husband, Verne;
to Denise, Brian, and Peggy;
and to the many people who shared their ideas
on how to channel stress more positively.

Contents

Creative Relaxation

Introduction

There are many books available today that describe stress. Most of them emphasize how stress is related to illness. *Creative Relaxation* differs from these. It gives us a new technique that goes beyond describing stress. In this book I will guide you through each of the active steps involved in learning the skill of Creative Relaxation. You will learn not only to identify stress and its effects on your life, but also to act positively to alleviate the problems caused by mischanneling stress. You will also gain skill in learning how to confront stress and transform it into a useful motivating force in your life. All the Creative Relaxation experiences used as examples in this book come from case histories of clients who have learned successfully to channel their stress. As you become proficient in managing your own stress, you will gain insights into how to avoid transferring your stress to others.

In much of the literature available on stress, few authors attempt to translate their intellectual theories into specific programs suited to the immediate needs of individuals living under stress. Theory is not enough. This book approaches stress from a practical point of view. I don't think that anyone can follow a few rigidly standardized steps based on theories and expect to succeed in channeling his or her highly personal stress.

Handling stress productively is a skill which you can acquire if you want to. This involves learning to identify the "stressor"—the stimulus that creates stress—and learning to channel this stress into positive energy. Environmental, social, and personal stressors are not imaginary. Simply pretending that they do not exist will not make them disappear.

The vehicle for learning how to channel your own stress positively is Creative Relaxation. This book is not a prescription. Creative Relaxation does not force you to disregard your own preferences and life-style. Creative Relaxation requires only that you understand the practical conditions under which you live and that you choose the most effective places in your life to apply a relaxation technique designed especially for your stress needs and life habits. While you learn Creative Relaxation, the emphasis is on what is most efficient and effective for you instead of what is right or wrong, good or bad. This skill is based on your active participation in determining how, when, and where in your life to benefit from the technique.

Creative Relaxation might be defined as a highly personalized system that enables an individual to channel stress in more positive ways by learning to become physically and emotionally relaxed and mentally refreshed. Once you learn the technique, you can benefit from practicing it at any time. It does not require special clothing, exercise, equipment, diet, or classes. It differs from other relaxation methods such as Transcendental Meditation, yoga, Zen meditation, conditioned relaxation, and desensitization in that you can use and benefit from practicing the technique at any time you are faced with the stresses from everyday situations. Creative Relaxation is a tool that you can use, for example, when a distressed customer explodes into your office, or when you play (and lose) the game of "Beat the Clock" on the freeway. Creative Relaxation also enables you to handle the inevitable disappointments of life, as when you plan to bask in the warm sun during your vacation, only to find continued cold and rainy weather. In addition, Creative Relaxation adapts to meet your changing moods, thus minimizing the boredom that often results when using the repetitive programs of other techniques. In this way, Creative Relaxation continues to meet your needs even as your life conditions change.

Creative Relaxation is purposefully designed to be easily incorporated into your life-style. For example, a nurse with three children has found that the best time to do Creative Relaxation is before leaving work at the end of the day. She comes home refreshed and is easily able to switch into her role as wife and mother. Another person has found that an ideal time to experience the technique is while driving to work. He is able to remain calm and easily takes that "early-morning glow" into the office with him.

Creative Relaxation is a skill. It is a vehicle to help you reach certain goals. In itself, Creative Relaxation will not make you a successful person in your career or your personal life. It *will* help you accomplish your goals by putting you in a better physical, emotional, and mental state.

Creative Relaxation is practiced in two ways. The first way is by experiencing a Personal Quiet Time. The Personal Quiet Time centers on mentally visualizing yourself in the most pleasant and ideal setting. Your own imagination becomes your tour guide for creating the "ideal environment" as you use the accompaniment of soothing musical or environmental sounds to help you create a comfortable scene. You focus on each of the various muscle groups within your body, starting with your toes and progressing all the way to your face. During this time your mind is free to allow thoughts to enter easily and leave spontaneously.

The second way that the technique is practiced is by integrating the sense of calmness and relaxation that results from the Personal Quiet Time into your busy, active day. In other words, you do not have to remove yourself from life's stressors in order to benefit from using the technique.

The Personal Quiet Time is divided into five Progressions in order to facilitate learning the method. Each Progression is designed to help you get more in touch with yourself physically, mentally, and emotionally. Progressions I and II emphasize the importance of becoming aware of the feelings associated with a muscle when it is tense and when it is relaxed. Progressions III and IV place greater emphasis on relaxing your mind and calming your emotions while continuing to relax the body. Each Progression provides increasing freedom for you to adapt the technique to your individual preferences. It is for that reason that Progression V, rather than being the end of the Personal Quiet Time, is the beginning. You are then ready to continue to use the technique as a tool to help you cope with the frustrations of more stressful times.

This logical and practical approach to handling stress needs to be learned and practiced. I will guide you throughout the book, helping to fit the technique to your needs and to assist you in better coping with many specific everyday stresses.

The first four chapters teach you how to obtain the mental, emotional, and physical benefits of practicing the technique. Later chapters serve as a guide in applying Creative Relaxation to different life situations. This book is built on the premise that its readers are in good health. Any plan to improve the quality of your life should begin with consulting your family physician.

Many publications on stress ask the reader to concentrate on "me, me, me." But it is lonely being the only person in the world. This book will help you live more comfortably with yourself, to work more effectively with your colleagues, and to be more open to sharing the world with those you love.

1 ❋ Stress

Stress has always been a basic—and necessary—part of human life; it is nothing new. What makes it seem different today is the complexity of our lives and the rapid changes to which we all must continuously adapt. Many times the stresses that affect us overlap and intertwine, making it difficult for us to determine their sources.

Many people think of stress negatively, as anything that makes them nervous, tense, upset, anxious, or angry. These may all be considered examples of stress, but perhaps they are better described as *distress*. Stress should be understood more broadly, even positively. It is more than reacting negatively to everyday frustrations. In fact, stress is not only a normal but an essential response.

Dr. Hans Selye of the University of Montreal, a leading authority on stress, defines it as the body's nonspecific response to any demand made upon a person. In other words, stress is the sum of adaptive changes that your body makes to help you adjust to various social or environmental situations. It is like temperature: you respond to hot temperatures just as you respond to cold temperatures. In the same way, you respond to positive demands as well as negative ones.

Stress is not synonymous with anxiety or tension. *Anxiety* is a fear reaction to some unknown cause. It is often your body's first response to any sudden change in your life. *Tension* is the contraction or tightening of the muscles in your body, whether voluntary or involuntary. When your muscles are not contracted, they are relaxed.

The concept of stress can be more clearly understood by taking a closer look at one day in the life of George, a competent, conscientious businessman, as well as a loving and attentive husband and father. Like everyone else, he sometimes experiences one of those days when nothing seems to go right. For George, such a day began when he couldn't find some legal papers necessary for a meeting with an important client. After frantically searching the house, he found his papers, but the search caused him to leave for work fifteen minutes later than usual. Trying to make up for lost time, he pressed his foot just a little harder on the accelerator. Unfortunately, he had failed to notice a radar-equipped police car until it pulled alongside him and its driver motioned him to the curb. George couldn't argue when the police officer chided him for traveling sixteen miles an hour over the posted speed limit. The time he lost while waiting for the ticket to be written out meant that he arrived at his office almost half an hour late. As it happened, his first appointment didn't show up anyway, and the client had neglected to call George's secretary to say he wouldn't be coming.

George made it through most of his working day without encountering anything worse than the usual frustrations. But thirty minutes before he could breathe a sigh of relief and head for home, his boss dashed into his office with a rush job that simply had to be done. It was an important project, absolutely vital to the company. Two hours later, George finally climbed wearily into his car and returned home. As soon as he opened the door, he was greeted by a fuming wife, three angry children, and an overcooked dinner that seemed to be made up exclusively of the foods he hated most. George had forgotten to call home and let his wife know he'd be working late.

You will probably agree that George experienced a great amount of stress. Let's look more closely at the specific stress reactions that his body underwent when he got the speeding ticket.

George reacted to the stressful event of the traffic ticket both cognitively and emotionally. The instant he saw the police car, he became fearful and anxious. As soon as he was sure he was going to be stopped, several thoughts raced through his brain. With lightning speed he considered possible ways of avoiding the ticket, as well as the consequences of getting it. By the time the police officer had actually leaned down to talk to George through his car window, George had begun to worry about the possible consequences of his lateness, and his fear was beginning to change to anger and frustration. Part of his anger arose simply from getting caught, and he was frustrated because he had no real choice about how to handle the matter. He had already decided that any argument with the police officer would only make matters worse.

George's responses were also physical. As soon as he saw the police officer signal him to pull over, he became aware that his heart was pounding. He felt a tightening in his chest, his breathing became rapid and choppy, and his hands were cold and sweaty, even trembling. There seemed to be a knot forming in his stomach. Other less noticeable signs were that George's heart and blood pressure were stimulated along with his muscles and lungs. The outcome was improved oxygen consumption, blood flow, and strength. Simultaneously the liver, spleen, and other necessary organs were activated, while still others, such as the digestive system, were inactivated.

These physical changes were the ultimate result of messages coming from George's hypothalamus, a region in the brain located at the base of the skull. The hypothalamus had stimulated the sympathetic nerves and the pituitary gland. The latter discharged ACTH (adrenocorticotrophic hormone), triggering an outpouring of adrenaline from the adrenal glands.

George's case illustrates the link between the emotional responses of fear, anger, and worry and the physical reactions that we associate with stress. Stress theorists such as Walter B. Cannon refer to these "stress reactions" as man's natural way to prepare himself for "fight or flight," a carryover from the times when physical struggle and speedy escape were the only alternatives in a moment of danger.

The fight-or-flight mechanism is helpful because it gears the body for effort and protects it from harm. The changes produced by the adrenals and the rest of the stress reaction mobilize the body's defenses. The response goads us into action.

The agent or stimulus that causes us to react is called a *stressor*, while the reaction to it is *stress*. For example, when the sun is the stressor, your skin reveals stress by becoming inflamed and painful. Often the complexities of modern life make it difficult for us to separate and identify individual stressors.

There are stressors of the natural life cycle—the frustrations of infantile dependency, of the adolescent's struggle for independence and identity, and of the physical limitations in advancing age. Disease and accidents are another common kind of stressor. Other more general types that directly affect most of us are those "landmark" life events—the beginning of formal schooling, graduating from school, entering the job market, getting married, going on vacation, and getting a job promotion. Then there are the stressors that we face in daily living—getting stuck behind a slow driver on the expressway, dropping a jar of mayonnaise on the floor you just waxed, watching your favorite football team lose a game.

Each time you are exposed to a stressor, your body reacts even if the stressor is positive. Take, for instance, a woman whose husband has given her a gorgeous full-length mink coat. Even though she is thrilled with the gift, she may immediately start to worry about getting insurance coverage and finding a place to store the coat. She also wonders if her husband will be willing to go out with her to luxurious places so that she can show off the coat. And she is concerned about getting a new wardrobe to match the status of the coat.

What makes the concept of stress even more complex is the uniquely human capacity to interpret the environment. When we add our interpretations to the existing stressors in daily living, we increase or decrease the impact of stress. Perceptions of stress can alter the impact of stress, but this does not mean that if we ignore or do not respond to a stressor that it goes away. This ostrichlike approach to stress is dangerous because the early signs of damaging stress responses often develop unnoticed. It is always better to develop skills to handle problems than to assume you can evade stress problems over a whole lifetime.

People are capable of mentally producing stressors by the way they perceive what is going on around them. A typical example of such self-created stressors is the act of driving the car with the gas gauge on empty. Some people think it's a game to be played by seeing how far they can go. Others are not enthusiastic about playing that kind of game; for them it is a real stressor. The way a person talks about situations can create stressors. Some common phrases are "I've got enough to worry about," "I've got more problems now than I know how to deal with," and "Life would be great if it weren't for all these problems." A classic phrase is "I will worry all night (day, week) until I find out." Many people are unaware of the stressor that is created by the way they speak. For instance, when you label a situation as a "problem" you are in fact producing for yourself an unpleasant stressor. Other potential "man-made" stressors are being seen in public with a run in your stocking, walking out of the house unshowered or without makeup, misspelling words in a letter, or seeing a dirty cup in the sink.

Man's perception of his environment in combination with the way he reacts is important to his level of efficiency, his effectiveness, and his overall health. According to Dr. Hans Selye, each time you react to a stressor, pleasant or unpleasant, you use a certain amount of your "adaptive energy supply." Dr. Selye contends that each of us is born with a certain finite supply of adaptive energy in order to adjust. Each time you use up some of your adaptive energy, it cannot be replaced. When your supply is depleted, death follows.

You can think of your adaptive energy supply as a savings account. The savings account is unique in that you can only *withdraw* from your account. Each time you react to a stressful situation, you use some of your adaptive energy, just as when you withdraw money from your savings account. How you spend your money and the size of your withdrawals are your own choice, just as it is your decision to determine how you use your supply of adaptive energy.

Another way to look at your adaptive energy supply is to compare it to fuel in a car. At birth your supply of adaptive energy is like a full gas tank in a car. Each time you experience stress, you use energy just as the car burns gasoline. When your supply is gone, your body is no longer able to adapt and it ceases to function, just as the car must coast and come to a stop when its tank is empty.

The analogy between your body and a car is useful to help clarify why it is important to learn to use your adaptive energy efficiently. The mileage that you get from your tank of gas depends on how you choose to drive your car. If you raced your motor at every stoplight, accelerated as rapidly as possible, and drove everywhere at top speed, your fuel supply would be quickly exhausted. You might get to where you wanted to go more quickly, but you would do so very wastefully. An alternative would be to conserve your gasoline as much as possible, for example, by never driving over thirty miles an hour. However, that would not be practical. You would be severely restricted in your travel. You would not have access to most freeways because of their minimum speed of forty-five miles an hour, and you certainly could never pass another car or have the power to pull out of close-call situations.

One of the most costly and wasteful situations is the tremendous expenditure of energy without getting anywhere at all. Many times people confuse motivation with motion. Getting angry at long check-out lines in the supermarket, becoming extremely nervous before an important meeting, or feeling frustrated by a broken television set are all examples of such negative or "dead-end" reactions. Directing anger to a useless target both wastes energy and delays action to defuse a stressor. Our friend George is a good illustration of wastefully channeled energy. He equates being conscientious with worrying. Each evening he brings home memories of the day's events and worries about them. As he looks forward to tomorrow, he also worries about what might happen then. Every time George is promoted, he finds more to worry about. In fact, it is almost as if he equates worrying with productivity, believing that anyone who doesn't worry must be "unwilling to pay the price for success."

There is no question that George is "paying his dues." Over a period of time he will wastefully deplete his supply of adaptive energy, and the wear and tear on his body will be great. For all this expended energy he will have traveled no farther along the road toward his life goals. What the payoff may be down the road is some form of disability or disease. He may not be able to enjoy his goals even if he does attain them. When stress persists over a long enough period of time, or if the stress reaction itself is severe enough, the body's ability to adapt becomes impaired.

For many people certain areas of the body are more vulnerable to stress. Exposure to stressors results in channeling or focusing the stress in these areas. For example, one of my clients became aware that whenever he had a disagreement with his wife, he tightened the muscles in his neck, back, and stomach. If his reaction to the argument was intense enough or if the argument continued for some time, he invariably walked away with a headache, a backache, and an upset stomach.

Stress that is channeled in negative ways is called distress. More of your adaptive energy supply is needed to respond in negative ways. Channeling stress negatively on a daily basis is costly, and it has a cumulative effect over a period of time.

People who channel stress negatively do not function at their optimal levels of productivity. For instance, it is not uncommon for a person who channels stress poorly to be exhausted by early evening during the week. On the weekend, he needs to sleep in. When faced with a crisis situation, he is not able to think clearly. Instead, he panics. After the crisis is over, he reviews his reactions, hoping that he did not make any mistakes.

The most common negative stress reactions serve as an early-warning system for stress damage to the body. They include tightness in the chest, rapid or pounding heartbeat, irritability, difficulty falling asleep, lack of concentration, upset stomach, tightness in the neck and shoulders, nagging headaches, dry mouth, sweaty palms, back pain, and clenched jaw.

As stress continues to build and is channeled improperly, more damage signs appear. Examples of more advanced stages of stress reactions are frequent inability to fall asleep, difficulty sleeping throughout the night, increased smoking or drinking, inability to unwind or switch roles at the end of the day, frequent headaches, constant stomach pain, thumping heart sounds, hyperventilation, and frequent lack of patience.

Over a long time the accumulated effects of negatively channeling stress eventually deplete one's supply of adaptive energy. The usual outcome is either illness or disease. Serious stress reactions can include migraine headaches, ulcers, high blood pressure, alcoholism, drug addiction, heart disease, asthma, and hay fever.

Many of life's stressors are out of your control. However, you always have the choice to decide how you want to react. The way we react to situations is basically learned. If you grew up in a family in which problems were always considered a "pain in the neck," it is not surprising that you suffer from neck pain. Similarly, if one of your parents always responded to an uncomfortable situation by saying, "Don't make me any more upset, you're causing my blood pressure to rise," then you may suffer from hypertension. Other examples of learned behavior include hearing "You make me sick" or "You give me a headache," after which you might get sick or develop a migraine. "You're driving me crazy" (or "to drink") may be said in part as a joke, but if you find such phrases coming true, then you know they are no longer funny.

If negative responses to stress are learned, then they can be unlearned, and more positive ways of reacting can take their place. Remember, you can change stress in terms of its quantity and quality. You cannot make it disappear.

The next chapter introduces you to the vehicle for learning how to channel stress effectively: Creative Relaxation.

2 ❋ Learning
to Use
Creative Relaxation

In Chapter 1 stress was identified as a natural response that humans have always experienced. If stress is nothing new, why is it talked about so much today? One characteristic that distinguishes life today from earlier times is rapid change.

Alvin Toffler in his book *Future Shock* dramatically points out that if we were to divide the 50,000 years of human life on earth into lifetimes of 62 years each, we would have approximately 800 lifetimes. Of those 800 lifetimes, 650 have been spent in caves. Most of human progress has occurred within the last 150 lifetimes.

The printed word has existed within the last six lifetimes, and only in the last four has it been available to the masses. The electric motor, a necessity today, has been available only within the last two lifetimes. Modern life then can be characterized by the rapid influx of new discoveries and inventions. We are all under constant pressure to adapt to these new and, at times, consternating discoveries.

Another example of our rapidly changing times is the

speed with which new ideas penetrate the homes of millions of families. Robert B. Young at Stanford Research Institute investigated the amount of time between the first commercial appearance of a new electrical product and the time the manufacturing industry that produced it reached peak production.

He first looked into items that were introduced before 1920. An electrical appliance like the electric range, the vacuum cleaner, or the refrigerator took an average of thirty-four years from the time it was first introduced on the market until it reached peak production. Young then researched the amount of time needed for a product to reach peak production between 1939 and 1959. He found that products like the television set, washer-dryer combination, and electric frying pan took only eight years. That is a 76 percent shrinkage. The significance of all this change is that we must react to new ideas in some way whether we desire the change or not.

Frequently we become so impressed with all of the brilliant accomplishments of modern technology that we tend to forget that our bodies continue to respond in primitive ways. When you and I feel threatened or sense danger, our bodies instantly react. This primitive response that prepares our body to defend itself is the natural fight-or-flight mechanism mentioned earlier. However, this response today is not always as appropriate as it once was. For example, when George was stopped by the police officer, his body instantly activated the fight-or-flight response. What this means is that George's body was prepared either to hit the police officer or to flee—simply leaving the police officer standing there alone. In either case the consequences would be severe. Instead, George had to sit there and stew in his own body's reactions.

Another familiar situation may elicit this response. You

are at a meeting and the chairman of the meeting begins to express views on a particular issue that are in conflict with yours. As you sit in your chair, your body prepares itself for fight or flight. Again, you must sit there and stew in your own body's reactions. It is amazing that stress reactions, even violent ones, occur anywhere from ten to fifty times in an average day, according to Dr. Jerry R. Day.

Practicing Creative Relaxation is important today because it gives your body a chance to replenish itself when bombarded by these daily stress reactions. But the technique of Creative Relaxation is important to modern man in an additional way. Creative Relaxation, when properly used, can help to rechannel stress in positive ways.

Creative Relaxation is a personalized approach to coping with the stresses of everyday living. Mastery of the technique will enable you to use it in the ways and at the times and places most suited to your particular needs. Unlike programs that require you to practice the technique by removing yourself from everyday stressful situations, Creative Relaxation is always available for you to use when you need it.

The best way to learn to use any new tool or to become proficient in a new skill is to approach it systematically. Like any other tool, Creative Relaxation becomes more helpful to you the more expert you become in handling it. You will find that learning the basics of the technique is enjoyable and uncomplicated. The challenge that most people face is not learning the technique, but practicing the technique daily on a habitual basis.

A person learns to practice and use the technique of Creative Relaxation in two ways. The first way is by learning the Personal Quiet Time. During the Personal Quiet Time you remove yourself from the rapid pace of a day and enjoy investing fifteen to twenty minutes alone with yourself. The

Personal Quiet Time is practiced in either a sitting or a lying position. During this time you mentally place yourself in the most pleasant scene, accompanied by soft musical and environmental sounds, as you concentrate on each of the muscle groups throughout your body, starting with your toes and progressing to your face. Thoughts are easily able to enter and leave your mind.

The second way that Creative Relaxation is practiced is by learning to transfer the calm and relaxed feelings that resulted from the Personal Quiet Time into your busy, active day. In other words, you do not have to remove yourself from a stressful situation in order to benefit from using the technique.

During the first night of an introductory workshop in Creative Relaxation, one tall, handsomely dressed executive asked me in a harsh voice if this technique would help him when he has an angry client in his office. He obviously could not stand there and close his eyes and imagine some utopia or picture himself in a pleasant scene. He sternly asked if this technique could realistically help him deal with such stressful situations. I said that I couldn't guarantee him that he could effectively use Creative Relaxation at those times. However, I reassured him that people who had that type of goal were successful.

This chapter will train you in learning each of the five Progressions, or steps, in the Personal Quiet Time. Chapters 3 and 4 will give you the necessary skills for learning to integrate the technique into your busy day.

PERSONAL QUIET TIME

The Personal Quiet Time—PQT for short—is practiced by removing yourself from your daily activities. This step differs from the later steps that can be used anywhere and anytime. It is the time you set aside for yourself and only yourself. You will need to set aside two twenty-minute periods each day.

It is very important that you don't regard the technique as a chore or an inconvenience. Your PQTs should become a part of your daily routine. They should become a pleasant habit, just like sitting down each day to enjoyable meals. Although some people at first find incorporating the habit easy, others tell me that they don't have the time. If this is your problem, the first thing you need to do is make the time. I suggest that people schedule it in their day just as they do any other important meeting. Your day is typically filled with numerous activities and responsibilities. In order for you to develop a habit of taking two twenty-minute periods to practice your PQT, you will need to select times that you can reasonably expect to have available regularly. For example, some people, because of their busy schedules, have actually "created" their own consistently available time. They wake up twenty minutes earlier each morning in order to practice the technique. In addition to scheduling a morning time, many people are benefiting from practicing the PQT later in the afternoon, perhaps just before they leave the office or before beginning to prepare the evening meal. After you have become thoroughly familiar with Creative Relaxation, you may wish to choose a time that comes right before a common daily stress situation.

One professional woman told me that she found it hard to switch gears after working all day in the office. As soon as she came home, she was bombarded by her children's demands, by cooking, and by all of the other things that had to be done. For this woman, practicing the Personal Quiet Time just before she went home helped her to change roles more easily from career woman to homemaker.

In fact, many homemakers find that a PQT is a great way to prepare before the kids get home from school. On the other hand, a business executive discovered that one of his best times for practicing PQT was during lunch. He not only felt more refreshed as a result of Creative Relaxation, but he also lost some unwanted pounds. The criterion for selecting the times to practice the PQT is that it most conveniently fits into your daily schedule and that it provides you with the most benefit.

The Personal Quiet Time for many people has grown to symbolize a time in which one "doesn't have to top anything or outdo anyone." It is a time when people can restore their bodies that have been drained from all of the daily pressures and come away feeling more refreshed and alert. One person described the feeling as being "like taking a shower without water." Many people have learned to associate the PQT as a time to calmly take inventory of oneself. The feelings you experience and the significance that the PQT plays in your life are as individual and unique as you are. The important thing to remember is to *practice* the Personal Quiet Time without fail.

Basic Guidelines for Your Personal Quiet Time

1. Be Alone

Ideally, you should be entirely alone. This period is an opportunity to be with yourself, and it is particularly important to avoid external associations or disruptions while you are learning Creative Relaxation. If you can, choose a time when you will not be likely to be interrupted. Then take your phone off the hook and ask your secretary to hold all calls for twenty minutes. Keep in mind that some telephones make a buzzing sound when they are left off the hook. In this case, go to a room away from the phone. Remember, too, that not all distractions are caused by other people. Such simple devices as wearing comfortable clothing and emptying your bladder before beginning your Personal Quiet Time can also help. For example, you may want to kick off your shoes, loosen your tie or belt, and remove your contact lenses or glasses.

2. Establish an Ideal Environment

Select a location that will enhance your PQT—for example, a favorite room—and then enhance it further by playing the kind of music (preferably instrumental) that you find particularly soothing. You may simply turn on your favorite radio station. (One woman even told me that she could listen to the news on the radio and still relax!) Sit or lie down comfortably, and feel free to change position at any time if it makes you more comfortable. You may even want to have a clock nearby. It is perfectly all right to check the time during this period.

3. Imagine an Ideal Scene

As you experience your PQT, allow your mind to create the kind of scene that you find most soothing. For example, you might think of an ocean scene at sunset, of lying under huge oak trees, or of being in an elegantly furnished and extremely comfortable hotel room. Some people find it easiest to picture a favorite place they once visited. One woman told me that she imagined many scenes with the help of pictures she had looked at in magazines. The point to remember is that the scene you create is your own, and it can be as simple or luxurious as you like, as long as it is comfortable for you.

Remember, do not make any association with anyone or

anything else when you place yourself in your scene. You should be alone, without your spouse, children, girlfriend or boyfriend. This is your time to be with yourself.

4. Let Your Thoughts Come and Go

As you place yourself in your ideal scene, allow thoughts to enter and leave your mind. It is not necessary for you to deal with your thoughts or evaluate them during your PQT. It is your time to let your thoughts and feelings emerge freely but nonjudgmentally. Whenever you realize you are concentrating on a thought, easily let it go by returning your focus of attention to the muscle group in your body where you left off.

5. Evaluate Yourself after the Personal Quiet Time

It is not necessary for you to evaluate how well you are relaxing during the twenty-minute period. There is no success or failure. The twenty-minute period is something you simply experience. For example, if you are relaxing a particular muscle group and you don't feel you are relaxing well enough, don't worry about it. Simply remind yourself that this is your nonevaluative time and move on to the next muscle group. You will find that by not dwelling on a particular area you can relax more readily.

Many people at first misunderstand what they are expected to feel as a result of Personal Quiet Time. It is not unusual to feel nothing has happened, but this is because the feelings associated with relaxation are different from anything else you experience on a daily basis. The feelings are not readily identifiable. When you exercise, for example by playing a vigorous game of tennis, your body's reactions are apparent. You breathe faster and harder, your heart pumps more rapidly, and you begin to perspire. Afterward your mind feels clearer and your muscles are tired; you are sweaty and thirsty for something cool. Your body's reactions to the Creative Relaxation technique, however, are more subtle. Your muscles are relaxed, and your breathing and pulse rate are lower instead of higher. Your body is still and calm.

People sometimes misinterpret these subtler reactions as an indication that the technique isn't working, or that they've done something wrong, but they shouldn't. Do not evaluate your progress during your PQT. Too often at the end of the twenty-minute period someone might say something like: "I couldn't believe it! I felt completely relaxed —except for the muscles in the lower portion of my left leg." This is a perfect example of continuing to evaluate. If you choose to judge and evaluate, do so only *after* you have returned to your active daily routine.

The Technique

You are now ready to begin a systematic, progressive approach to Creative Relaxation. Having chosen your Personal Quiet Times and familiarized yourself with the basic guidelines you should follow during each period, you will use these times to practice the five Progressions that lead to mastery of the technique. Progressions I and II can be called the *physical* Progressions, because through them you will learn to remove yourself from the stress and activity of your daily routine by concentrating on the various muscle groups in your body. Progression I is highly structured, for you will be instructed how to tighten and relax your muscles in a particular order. Progression II is less structured. Although you will again contract and relax specific muscle groups, you can vary and select the way you contract them.

Progression III can be called the *mental* Progression, because it involves more of your emotions and thoughts than Progressions I and II. Since you will have become adept at physical relaxation through the process of contracting a muscle first and then relaxing it, this Progression involves achieving the same relaxed sensations in your muscles more quickly, by eliminating the step of contracting them. Consequently, Progression III focuses on relaxing your mind and expanding your level of consciousness. In addition, you will begin to identify those times or events in your daily life that are most stressful for you.

Progression IV is the creative Progression. At this stage you will create your own method of Creative Relaxation. You will learn how to select and coordinate the components of each of the three previous Progressions that will best suit your needs. You will practice varying the elements of your Personal Quiet Time to complement your mood. And finally, you will learn to use and benefit from Creative Relaxation during those times of your day that you have learned to identify as stressful.

Progression V is the advanced Progression. Learning the Personal Quiet Time is a skill, and like any skill it must be practiced. Over a period of time you will be able to relax your body more quickly and easily. The fifth Progression will show you how.

Now that you are ready to begin Progression I, it is important that you remember to follow each of the basic guidelines outlined above every time you practice your Personal Quiet Time. Let me review them briefly for you:

1. Be alone; do not make any association with anyone or anything else.
2. Establish an ideal environment; choose a place that is quiet and comfortable, and play soothing music if you wish.

3. Imagine an ideal scene; make it as luxurious and idealized as you like.
4. Let your thoughts come and go freely.
5. Do not evaluate your progress.

Progression I: Physical Relaxation with Specific Guidelines

Practice this Progression twice daily, preferably in the morning and afternoon, for three to five days. Do not move on to Progression II until you have thoroughly learned how to contract and relax your muscles according to the instructions.

1. Lie down comfortably. Close your eyes and feel yourself breathing, inhaling and exhaling smoothly and rhythmically.
2. While continuing your rhythmical breathing, imagine a scene that pleases you for the moment. (In order to illustrate the technique, I will assume that you have imagined an ocean scene, but you should imagine the setting most attractive to you.) See the ocean, with the waves gently rolling up to the shore, and the beach whose silken sand has been warmed by the rays of the slowly setting sun.
3. As you imagine this scene, place yourself in it. See and feel yourself lying on luxurious sand. Feel the warmth that radiates from the sand, and how it begins to relax you. Feel the gentleness of the ocean breeze as it passes over your body—it is just cool enough to make the warm sand even more relaxing. Hear the rhythmical sounds of the waves as they roll up onto the shore and back out to sea.
4. Once you are completely comfortable on your

beach, concentrate on the muscles in your left foot. Contract these muscles by pointing your toes down toward the floor, as if you were pointing them into the sand. Tighten them as hard as you can and *hold* them for a slow count of three. Release and relax.

While you perform these actions, say or think to yourself: "I feel my toes uncurling. I feel the softness and smoothness of each grain of sand between my toes as they continue to relax. The muscles in my left foot feel so limp that I have no desire to move."

5. Concentrate on the muscle in your left calf. Contract the muscle by bringing your toes back and pointing them toward your face. Tighten and *hold* for a slow count of three. Release and relax.

As you relax the muscle, say to yourself: "I feel the tension drifting off and the muscle becoming loose. The warmth of the sun helps me to relax."

6. Concentrate on the muscles in the upper portion of your left leg. Contract them by pushing your heel into the floor as hard as you can. *Hold* for a slow count of three. Release and relax.

Continue to imagine the soothing sensations associated with the ocean, the breeze, and the warm sand and how they continue to calm you.

7–9. Repeat the same sequence for each of the three muscle groups in your right foot and leg.

10. Concentrate on the muscles of your buttocks. Contract them by squeezing them together as hard as you can. *Hold* for a slow count of three. Release and relax.

As you perform these actions, say to yourself: "I am nestling my body into the sand. The sand is shaping itself to the conformation of my body, and it cradles me as I relax into it." At this point reflect back to the muscles in the lower portion of your body. Notice the overall relaxed feeling and how you can sense the warm sand. You should have no desire to move.

11. Concentrate on the muscles in your abdomen. Contract them by inhaling and pushing your stomach out as far as you can. *Hold* for a slow count of three. Slowly exhale and relax.

    If you hear any rumbling noises in your abdominal area, don't worry. They are an indication that you are relaxing.

12. Pause and enjoy how easily thoughts are entering and leaving your mind. Just like the ocean waves, thoughts roll in and roll out, with no effort or difficulty.

    You may find yourself thinking a specific thought connected with your daily activities, as perhaps about a business worry or a household responsibility. In this case simply acknowledge the idea and return your concentration to the muscle group you have just reached. Continue to relax the muscles.

13. Concentrate on the muscles in your back. Contract them by inhaling and pushing your back into the floor. *Hold* for a slow count of three. Begin to relax, feeling the relaxation begin in the muscles in your lower back. The warmth of the sand helps them relax, and the warmth spreads to the middle portion of your back and then to the upper portion. You can feel each vertebra loosen as the warmth travels along your spinal column.

14. Concentrate on the muscles in your left hand.

Contract them by making a tight fist. *Hold* for a slow count of three. Release and relax.

Say to yourself: "I can feel the smooth sand under my fingertips, and each grain is warm and soothing. My entire hand is motionless and heavy with relaxation."

15. Concentrate on the muscles in your left arm. Contract them by opening your fingers and pushing your hand down into the floor as hard as you can. *Hold* for a slow count of three. Begin to relax, feeling the relaxation begin in the muscles of your lower arm and spread to your upper arm.

16–17. Repeat the same sequence for the muscle groups in your right hand and arm.

18. Concentrate on the muscle groups in your neck and shoulders. Contract them first on the left side, by lifting your shoulder and tilting your head toward it until they touch. Push them against each other. *Hold* for a slow count of three and slowly relax. Repeat the same sequence on the right side.

The neck and shoulder area is for many people the place where the tensions of the day seem to accumulate. Imagine that as you lie on the beach a wave laps softly against you. As it withdraws it seems to take the tensions with it. You can almost feel the shoulder and neck muscles lengthening as they relax.

19. Concentrate on the muscles in your neck. Contract them by bringing your head forward until your chin meets your chest. *Hold* for a slow count of three. Slowly relax your head to a comfortable position.

20. Pause and allow yourself to feel your entire body. It is as if you have settled completely into the

warm sand, which holds you so that you have no desire to move any part of your body.

21. Concentrate on the muscles in your face. Contract them by wrinkling your forehead, eyes, and mouth. *Hold* for a slow count of three. Release and relax. The cool breeze is brushing the wrinkles from your face, and your eyelids are so heavy that you have no desire to open them. All of the facial expressions and mouth movements that you make during the day are smoothed away, and your jaw is relaxed.

22. Pause and become aware of your breathing. Continue to inhale and exhale smoothly and rhythmically. Notice the smoothness in each breath of air.

23. Again imagine the entire scene in which you have been progressively relaxing for the last fifteen minutes. Enjoy the deep sense of relaxation that you have been experiencing.

24. Count to five. Slowly open your eyes. Say to yourself, "Now that my journey is nearing an end, I will awaken in the usual manner, feeling more refreshed and revitalized."

25. Sit up. Remain sitting quietly for a minute or two. You may now resume your daily activities.

After you have practiced Progression I you may have some questions about what you have just experienced. Although it is important to remember not to evaluate yourself during your Personal Quiet Time, it is sometimes useful to do so afterward. First, identify your physical responses. Do you have an overall relaxed feeling? Have your thoughts slowed down? Check your breathing—does it feel smoother or faster and irregular? Feel the temperature in your hands and feet —are they warmer or colder? Are the palms of your hands sweaty or dry?

Some responses that indicate you have reached a relaxed state are warmth in your hands and feet, smooth, rhythmical breathing, dry hands, and clearer thoughts. If you have experienced any of these signs, then you are relaxing correctly. When one person said to me, "I was able to feel myself relaxing all of my muscles except my thigh muscles," I responded: "That's OK. Remember, you don't have to evaluate yourself during your Personal Quiet Time. The important thing is how you feel now."

Some people worry because they think they are unable to relax at all. Several individuals have told me they have an extremely difficult time "just lying there" for twenty minutes. They get more tense. If this is your problem, I suggest that you practice the Progression for only five or ten minutes and then get up. Repeat this procedure for three days, and then extend the time to fifteen minutes. Practice for another three to seven days, and by then you will probably be comfortable with extending your Personal Quiet Time to the full twenty minutes.

Other people worry about timing. They report that they go through the complete Progression in only ten minutes, and then are left wondering what to do. If this is also your problem, I make two recommendations. First, take a longer time imagining your pleasant scene. Take extra time to see yourself in the center of that scene, enjoying the ultimate comfort that it brings you. Second, increase the time you concentrate on each muscle group, perhaps simply by counting to five rather than three.

Some people worry about high blood pressure or heart disease. If you are hypertense or have heart disease, I recommend that you continue to breathe at a smooth and rhythmical pace as you contract each of the muscles in your body. Holding your breath as you contract them decreases the amount of blood flow back to your heart. (You might be interested to know that one of the prime functions of breathing, in addition to bringing oxygen into the body, is to help force the blood back to the heart.)

Finally, some people actually worry that they are relaxing too much. For example, one individual asked me: "I felt as if I drifted in and out of sleep the whole time. Is that all right?" I answered: "Of course, because Personal Quiet Time is entirely your own, and you should give your body what it needs during this time. However, if you continue regularly to fall asleep, perhaps you should sit up during your session. Furthermore, you should take another look at your daily routine. Falling asleep may be a signal that your body is sending you—are you overexerting during the day, or not getting enough sleep at night?" Other people, after experiencing Progression I, explain that they feel as if they have just awakened from a three- or four-hour nap. To them I explain that by unwinding with the Personal Quiet Time their bodies are telling them that they are overdriving themselves. Too often we push ourselves too hard. One of the first benefits of Creative Relaxation is that you too will discover if you have been demanding too much of yourself.

Progression II: Physical Relaxation with General Guidelines

This Progression builds on the knowledge of how to contract and relax specific muscle groups, but in it you will begin to experiment, incorporating variations on the basic technique outlined in Progression I. The general guidelines are only suggestions. Follow whichever of them work best for you. Practice this Progression for three to five days. Do not move on to Progression III until you have learned (1) how to tighten each of the muscles in your body effectively and comfortably and (2) how to recognize tension in specific muscles and be able to relax them at will after first contracting them.

1. Vary your position. As you practice, discover the posture most comfortable for you. Most people seem to prefer sitting with their hands lying comfortably in their laps, but you may choose to continue lying down as you did during Progression I. Individuals who suffer from lower back pain have found that lying on the floor on their backs with their knees bent and their feet flat on the floor is a perfect position.

2. Vary your scene. Rather than visualizing the ocean, waves, and a sandy beach, create a new but equally pleasing picture. For example, imagine a log cabin high in the mountains on a snowy afternoon. Place yourself in front of the fireplace, nestling into a fluffy rug and feeling the warmth of the crackling fire. As you proceed through each of the muscle groups, say or think key phrases, such as "I'm letting go," "unwinding," or "sensing a wave of a calm feeling," as you use this new scene to enhance your relaxation.

3. Vary the method by which you contract muscle groups. As you practice, you will discover that muscles may be contracted in different ways. For example, instead of making a fist to tighten the muscles in your hand, open it and extend your fingers as hard as you can. The muscles in your neck can be tensed differently by stretching them toward the opposite shoulder, causing the muscles to lengthen. You can also vary the way you tighten your jaw muscles. Instead of bearing down on your teeth, open your mouth as wide as possible.

Now that you have practiced Progression II, you may have some questions about what you have just experienced. Remember, it is important that you know how to relax your muscles. After you have tightened the muscles, consciously note the tension before you let that tension go.

Some people complain that contracting certain muscles makes them feel uncomfortable. I remind them that they can learn from an experience, even if it is one that doesn't seem pleasant. Recognizing and acknowledging how you feel is a significant part of learning to create your Personal Quiet Time. I recommend that you try a technique several times before you decide not to use it, because each experience will be different. What you dislike during one session may please you greatly the next.

Practicing each Progression several times will also help you to know more clearly what it is you like. You can use this knowledge to aid you in coping with more stressful times. For example, suppose that during your practice you have found that contracting your calf and thigh muscles is uncomfortable. Then one night you get into bed, knowing that tomorrow will be a very challenging day. You simply can't get to sleep because your mind is buzzing with thoughts about the coming day. Now is the time to call on those elements of Creative Relaxation that will help you relax and fall asleep, but you should not include contracting your thigh and calf muscles.

Other people worry about having difficulty imagining a scene. If you have this problem, one path toward visualizing a pleasant scene is to re-create in your mind a place that you once visited. One person found that it was easier to create a fanciful scene, and she visualized herself lying on top of creamy, white whipped cream floating in a giant cup of aromatic hot chocolate.

Another worry you may have is what to do if you are

distracted while practicing your Personal Quiet Time. For instance, one man told me after a session that he had gone through the entire twenty minutes enduring an itch on his back. When I asked him why he didn't scratch it, he replied that he was afraid to move. If you have an itch, go ahead and scratch it! Another type of distraction is one that comes from the outside world. If someone calls for you and it is not an emergency, say you will be there shortly. Take about thirty seconds to prepare yourself before getting up. This preparation is important, because your body is in a relaxed state, and if you jump up too quickly you may feel some dizziness or sluggishness.

Progression III: Mental Relaxation

This Progression continues the physical experiences of the two previous Progressions, but in it you will relax without first contracting your muscles. Practice this Progression for three to five days. Do not move on to Progression IV until you can easily relax your muscles without tightening them first, and until you can comfortably accept any thought that enters your mind, including those arising from stressful situations.

1. Close your eyes. Feel yourself breathing. Each time you inhale, let the air travel down to fill your abdomen, and continue to breathe in until your chest is filled with air. Exhale, feeling the air slowly escape as a wave all the way down to your pelvis.
2. Gradually relax all muscles. Follow the same sequence of muscle groups as you did in the previous Progressions, and try to achieve the same relaxed feelings associated with each muscle group without contracting them first.

You may find it helpful to repeat details of the pleasant scene you imagined in the first two Progressions. Another alternative is to use key words or phrases that trigger memories of soothing sensations. For example, you might think "letting go," "beginning to unwind," "waves of a calm feeling," "warmth and softness."

3. Open your mind. Because your conscious mind does not have to concentrate on contracting specific muscle groups, it will be available to any number of thoughts. Allow these thoughts to enter and leave freely. Some of them may involve stress or unpleasant ideas. You may find yourself thinking about your many responsibilities, about meeting an important client, or about a dentist's appointment, for example. Acknowledge your thoughts, but do not attempt to control them or to concentrate on any one particular idea.

4. Concentrate on your breathing.
5. Count to five. Slowly open your eyes.
6. Sit quietly for a minute or two.

Now that you have experienced Progression III, you may have some additional questions about the method. For example, some people are concerned about whether they are breathing properly. You may not be aware that breathing from the abdomen is a natural way of breathing that can have a very calming effect. The process of inhaling can be compared to filling a glass with water. As you draw air in through your nasal passages, it first fills your abdomen, just as the glass is filled with water poured in from the top. Exhalation is like emptying the glass. The air pours out from the top, beginning in your chest and continuing down to your pelvis. Your breathing should be smooth and rhythmical. I recommend that you begin by inhaling and exhaling on two counts and gradually increase the time to four counts.

Another concern people may have after they become more familiar with Creative Relaxation is whether the technique will interfere with other training programs. I can confidently tell them that over the years I have found that there is no interference. In fact, many people have returned to me to say that Creative Relaxation enhanced the effectiveness of other methods. For instance, in one case Creative Relaxation complemented a self-development program for business executives and managers. One executive attending this program had a difficult time achieving the various goals he had set for himself. After practicing Creative Relaxation, he realized that he was setting goals that someone else had told him to establish, not those that he himself wanted to achieve. The result was a happier man who was setting and meeting his own objectives.

Still other people are worried about learning how to let go of their thoughts. One woman said that she had little difficulty thinking thoughts—she considered the various chores she wanted to accomplish, a meeting she was going to attend, what she wanted to prepare for dinner. Her problem lay in being able to let the thoughts go. I told her that as soon as she realized she was concentrating on a particular thought, she should acknowledge it, but then replace it by focusing her attention on the specific muscle group she had reached in the Progression. Another technique she found effective was to visualize a tape recorder, with a reel of tape on which her thoughts were recorded. When she found herself holding on to a thought, she merely imagined turning on the machine and having the recorded thought move away. Remember, the number and kind of thoughts that enter your mind during your Personal Quiet Times will vary. The important thing is that you let them go.

On the other hand, you may find that you are scarcely conscious of time passing. One man explained to me that he checked the clock before practicing his Personal Quiet Time, but that after what he thought to be only a few minutes, his time was almost over. I assured him that when time seems to pass very quickly, your mind is probably not thinking on the conscious level. It is left free to entertain a multitude of thoughts, and that is desirable. You should always remember not to worry about how fast or how slowly time passes during your Personal Quiet Time.

One final question that people often ask me at this point is "When can I begin using the technique during stressful situations?" I always answer, "Before you can begin effectively to integrate Creative Relaxation into your daily lifestyle, you will have to identify the situations that are most stressful for you personally." Situations commonly mentioned to me include having to go to the gas station to fill up the car, having to wait in a check-out line at the supermarket, and getting into a petty argument at home before leaving for work. Women, in particular, increasingly mention the stress of having to adjust to new sets of responsibilities as they move between home and office.

A good way for you to begin to learn to identify situations that are stressful for you is to become more sensitive to your body's signals. For example, one executive complained about getting headaches. I told him to ask himself the following three questions the next time he got one: (1) What time did I first notice the headache? (2) What was I doing at the time? (3) What was I doing, or what had happened, previously? This man discovered that his headaches always developed while he was at the office doing paperwork. Furthermore, by paying attention to what his body was trying to tell him, he found that whenever he wrote for long periods of time he kept tightening the muscles in his neck and shoulders. The result, invariably, was a headache. By using the kind of recall process I recommended to this man, you will gain both greater awareness of the external factors that cause you daily tension and greater awareness of your own response to them.

You are ready to move on to Progression IV when you have identified situations that you consider stressful. Remember, a stressful situation can be positive as well as negative.

Progression IV: Creative Relaxation

This Progression involves learning two things. First, you select and coordinate all of the different components that have worked most successfully for you as you practiced Progressions I through III. Second, this Progression encourages you to apply those techniques discovered during the Personal Quiet Time to everyday stressful situations. The PQT has helped you develop many techniques by which you can feel comfortable. Now it is your turn to re-create that sense of comfort whenever you need it.

Creative Relaxation is designed to grow with you, and thus it is entirely open-ended. The guidelines presented here are suggestions about the kinds of choices you may make, but the choices you do make should be yours alone. Practice the PQT in Progression IV for three to five days. At the end of this period you will truly have reached a new beginning. You will be able to use the relaxed feelings you have created whenever you need them to cope with the frustrations and tensions of day-to-day living.

1. Choose the most effective components of your Personal Quiet Time. As you practiced Progressions I through III, you may have found that certain elements always worked well in helping you relax. For example, one individual might discover an ideal combination in lying down on his bed while soft piano music plays on the phonograph and in visualizing resting in a hammock beside a brook. If he varied one of these elements—perhaps by substituting vocal music for the piano instrumentals—he could still relax, but not as quickly or completely. Another person, however, might prefer to choose among several different positions, types of music, and types of scene, according to his mood on any given day. He might also choose to omit one component altogether, by experiencing his PQT in silence, or choosing not to visualize any scene at all. Varying the components of your PQT, of course, minimizes the boredom that can result from a too rigidly defined program.

2. Choose the most effective components of your muscle relaxation technique. Some people might prefer to return to the strictly ordered sequence of contraction and relaxation in Progression I, while others choose to vary the sequence, or simply relax their muscles in no particular order without contracting them first. It is especially effective to concentrate on relaxing those muscle areas where you most often feel strain in your daily life. For example, one businessman learned from Progression III to recognize that the muscles in his neck were always tight by the end of his workday, producing a tension headache. When he practiced the technique during

his Personal Quiet Time in the afternoon, he was able to relieve the headache by choosing specifically to contract and relax his neck muscles.

3. Identify stressors that arise from daily activities where Creative Relaxation is applicable. At the end of the day, identify at least one stressor and resolve it by using your most comfortable Creative Relaxation technique to channel your stress. One man who suffered tension headaches was, in time, able to transfer the relaxed feelings he achieved during his Personal Quiet Time to his neck muscles while he was actually working, face to face with the pressures that caused his original problem. Another executive learned to integrate the relaxed feelings from his Personal Quiet Time with his typically hectic morning schedule. He became less emotional and was able to think more rationally and clearly as he was being bombarded with questions and assignments. Even the people in his department noticed the improvement in his behavior.

A concern that many people have is whether you have to be alone to do the technique. Or could you do it, say, on the subway to and from work? Of course. The PQT is *experienced* alone but it can be *practiced* in the presence of other people. When you are first learning the technique, you will find it easier to practice the twenty-minute period alone and with a minimal number of distractions. As you become more proficient in the skill, you will find that interruptions and outside noises do not distract you as they may have in the beginning. For instance, you may be distracted by a sudden noise, but you will easily be able to return to your relaxed state.

An important question that is invariably asked at some

point is "What will happen if I don't have the full twenty minutes to practice my Personal Quiet Time? Should I do the technique or not?" Yes, you should.

The fifth Progression in the technique explains how you can practice the technique in only ten or fifteen minutes.

Progression V: Advanced State of Creative Relaxation

At this stage your body has learned to recognize the sensations and is familiar with the relaxed feelings of the Personal Quiet Time. Since you are more proficient at relaxing each of your muscles, you will be able to reach the same relaxed state quickly. You should be able to relax each muscle in your body regardless of whether the muscle is contracted first or not. This Progression can be practiced effectively in a shorter time because you are able to reach an overall relaxed state more quickly and easily.

Progression V involves contracting the entire musculature of your body at one time instead of relaxing individual muscle groups as you did in the previous Progressions. It is recommended that you use this Progression whenever you do not have the full twenty minutes to practice the other Progressions. Here is one way you can practice the technique in only ten or fifteen minutes:

1. Select a comfortable environment. If you desire, play your favorite musical or environmental sounds.
2. Close your eyes.
3. Begin breathing very smoothly and regularly, allowing the air first to enter your abdominal area. As you exhale, let the air exit from the top of your lungs, then gradually down to your stomach area.

4. Visualize in your mind a very pleasant scene.
5. Maximally contract all of the muscles in your body from your toes to your face. Hold for three counts and relax. (One man finds that it is easier for him to relax if he coordinates his muscle contraction with the scene he visualizes. For instance, the ocean scene is his favorite. When he imagines a wave rolling up onto the shore, he contracts his muscles. When the wave rolls back out, he begins loosening them.)
6. Systematically relax your muscles, starting with your left and right feet. As soon as they feel comfortable, relax the lower and upper portions of each leg.
7. Relax the muscles in your buttocks. As the muscles loosen, pause and notice how the muscles in the whole lower half of your body feel relaxed.
8. Sense the relaxation in your stomach area as the sensation spreads to the muscles in your back.
9. The muscles in your neck and shoulder area join in as you feel the tensions seeping away, leaving the muscles more relaxed. Reflect back to the luxuriousness of the scene and the relaxed feelings in your body.
10. Relax the muscles in your left and right hands. Feel the warmth from the spot where you lie helping to soothe and relax the muscles in your left and right arms.
11. Feel the muscles in the lower and upper portions of each arm loosening as you absorb the warmth from the spot where you lie.
12. Feel each of the muscles in your face loosening as the tensions easily drift away, leaving your muscles relaxed and comfortable.

13. Pause and become aware of your breathing. Focus on inhaling and exhaling for four counts.
14. Count to five. Say to yourself, "Now that my journey is nearing an end, when I reach five I will awaken in the usual fashion, feeling refreshed and revitalized."
15. Sit up and remain sitting quietly for a minute or two.
16. You may now resume your daily activities.

People ask me to explain more fully what I mean when I tell them that Progression V signals "a new beginning." I can best explain it by emphasizing that as you continue to grow in life and encounter new experiences, you can use and benefit from Creative Relaxation. For example, one woman decided to take up the game of racquet ball. Whenever it was her turn to hit the ball, she used to become very anxious. This caused her to contact the ball too early, resulting in an easy return shot for her opponent. She learned how to use Creative Relaxation to enable her to reduce her anxiety and tension, and now she is able to wait until the ball is at a lower point before hitting it. The consequence is a "kill" shot—and a point won. Another person learned how to benefit from Creative Relaxation when he began a new job. Each day he has a thirty-minute subway ride to and from work. He has learned how to practice his Personal Quiet Times during the trip, and he both enters his office and returns home feeling refreshed and invigorated.

By now you may be wondering exactly how you can go about practicing and benefiting from Creative Relaxation during your own everyday life. Chapter 3 is devoted to helping you learn this skill. Putting Creative Relaxation to its best use lies in making the right choices—you decide when, where, and how to use the technique. I can't promise you that Creative Relaxation will solve all of your problems or make you a success. You will never get rich solely by practicing the technique. You must still determine your life goals and how you want to achieve them. But Creative Relaxation will put you in a better physical and mental state and enable you to function at the top of your form as you go after the things you want in life. Creative Relaxation is to a man or woman what a smooth road is to a car. It will help you reach your goals more quickly and efficiently and you will arrive at your destination with less wear and tear on your body and your mind.

3 ❋ The Pendulum Concept of Stress

It is true that we create many of our stressors. Some of these stressors could be eliminated if we were able to lower our stress level. Once the tension level is lowered, we are in a much better position to handle a situation adequately.

As previously mentioned, this is important because mischanneling stress is costly to our overall well-being and to our ability to function optimally. The goal is not to avoid life's stressors but to learn how to react to them better. Creative Relaxation is the tool that enables us to channel stress more positively.

The next step to learning Creative Relaxation is to integrate the technique into your day. In order to accomplish this, it is important that you thoroughly understand the Pendulum Concept of stress. The Pendulum Concept is a six-step process that can be used in any situation to help you channel stress more positively. The "Pendulum" represents your reactions to a situation; it can swing in either a negative or a positive direction. When your reactions interfere with your ability to handle a situation adequately, the pendulum is in a negative position. To swing the pendulum from a negative to a positive position, you must first eliminate any negative stress reactions. Once the harmful effects of stress are negated, the pendulum can continue to swing in a more positive direction. The Pendulum Concept is based on the premise that just as you have learned to channel stress in negative ways, so can you learn to channel it in positive ways.

It is important to realize that channeling stress positively is a skill. It may take many forms. There is not one answer or magic formula for every stressful situation. The Pendulum Concept acts as a guide that enables you to deal effectively with the individual stresses of each situation. You will learn to swing your mental and physical state from a negative condition through a neutral state into a positive and energy-filled awareness of your own potential.

It is not necessary for you to use all six steps in each situation. Nor is it necessary for you to follow each of the six steps in sequence. Your goal is to use the skills from Creative Relaxation that are most efficient and effective for you. However, when you are attempting to deal with a difficult situation, it is recommended that you consider each of the six steps in sequence.

STEP 1. Know what you want. It is important to identify clearly what you want. This goes beyond determining long-term goals. It gets as specific as being aware of what you wish to achieve in such daily situations as having a conversation with another person, having your hair cut, buying clothes, or ordering food in a restaurant.

Many times people think they know what they want, when in reality they don't. The end result is disappointment and unhappiness. For one couple, the question of what to do for dinner clearly illustrates this point. During Creative Relaxation sessions, Mary realized that she frequently confused her desire to escape from very heavy housework with the desire to go out to eat. She would return home from the restaurant feeling dissatisfied and pressured because she still had too many things to do and not enough time to do them all. She learned through Creative Relaxation to acknowledge to herself what she really wanted. She learned to distinguish between not being in the mood to cook and wanting to eat out. Both she and her husband were more satisfied as a result.

Another important consideration is to determine specifically what you want from start to "finish." One client, Jane, quickly learned the importance of this. One evening Jane set the simple goal of going out for dinner. By the end of the evening she had achieved her goal, but she was miserable. Instead of going to a nice restaurant to eat, her husband brought her to a hamburger stand. Technically, she ate outside the house, but that was not the only thing she had wanted. Thus it is important to set your goals precisely. In our examples so far, setting goals has involved determining where a person wants to eat. At other times it may mean deciding what you want to eat.

If you do not decide specifically what you want, then you choose instead to leave yourself open to chance. Sometimes the outcome is positive, but more frequently it is disappointing. When you determine specifically what you want, you increase your chances of being satisfied at the end.

STEP 2. Become aware of your reactions. It is important to learn to listen to the type of reactions that your body has. Some common signs of negative reactions to stress include a tightening in the chest, an increase in blood pressure and heart rate, irregular breathing, sweaty cold palms, a knot in the stomach, and a tensing in the muscles in the neck and shoulders.

STEP 3. Identify the stressor. Steps 2 and 3 are frequently reversed, since there may be times when it is easier to associate feelings of being tense with specific stress reactions. Once the response is identified, you can take step 3—isolating the reaction to a stressor.

In some situations, however, the stressor may be recognized first. The specific stress reaction is unidentified. It is not until the specific stress reaction becomes severe enough that a person takes notice.

For Jack, who developed high blood pressure, the source of stress was the combination of a recent separation from his wife and considerable weight gain throughout the trauma of learning to accept bachelorhood. Jack was never aware that he was reacting in ways that would cause him to become hypertensive. However, once he received training in Creative Relaxation, he recognized that in stressful situations he would tighten the muscles in his chest and his heart would start pounding. Creative Relaxation in his case did not prevent him from developing high blood pressure, but it was effective, when used in conjunction with his medications, in lowering his blood pressure.

STEP 4. Evaluate the degree to which your reactions or behaviors due to stress are helping you attain what you want.

STEP 5. Determine whether you can eliminate the stressor. If you can remove the source of your stress, then it is necessary for you to develop several reasonable alternative plans of action that might change the stressor. For instance, suppose that you have determined that your boss creates a lot of stress for you at work. You can eliminate the stressor—the boss, in this case—by (1) quitting your job, (2) having a heart-to-heart talk with your boss, or (3) asking to be transferred to another department.

Once you have determined several reasonable plans of action, select one of the alternatives that will help you get what you want. It is then important that you take some action. Do not start by working on the most difficult thing first. Instead, work at your plan one step at a time. Redirect your energy into making an organized plan. Many people have found that when they invest some extra time to get organized, instead of rushing hurriedly into a situation, more time is saved. Once it is organized, the execution of the plan is made quicker and smoother.

STEP 6. Rechannel your reactions in a more positive direction when the stressor is still present. If you cannot eliminate the stressor, then it becomes necessary for you to make certain adjustments in the way you react.

The first step in swinging the stress pendulum in a positive direction is negating or neutralizing the negative stress reactions. This is accomplished by negating the body's overall reaction by neutralizing specific areas in your body. Here's one way to negate stress and eliminate that overall tense feeling:

1. Inhale very deeply and smoothly.
2. Hold for about three seconds.
3. As you slowly and evenly exhale, produce a wave of calm throughout your body, starting at your head and progressing all the way down to your feet.

Some people at first question whether this process for negating stress is noticeable to others. The answer is that it is not any more noticeable than sighing. The main difference is in the benefit one receives. Sighing produces a superficial, momentary feeling of relief. The process of negating stress relaxes the total musculature of the body. It helps the body to regain its equilibrium by neutralizing the negative reactions. This is important for two reasons: less adaptive energy is wasted, and at the same time, the various stress organs in the body do not work as hard. Conserving your adaptive energy and neutralizing the negative reactions to stressors will help you eliminate bad side effects such as stomach ulcers and nagging headaches.

Some people prefer to negate the overall negative reaction by imagining their favorite scene as they exhale, in place of creating the wave of calm. Others are successful in eliminating that all-over anxious feeling by (1) looking up at the ceiling as they smoothly inhale, (2) holding as before, and (3) exhaling while slowly counting to themselves from one to ten, and relaxing the muscles in their body as they count.

Many people funnel their responses to one area in their body. One common site is the stomach. You negate the negative stress by (1) inhaling fully and deeply, filling the lower part of the lungs near the stomach first; (2) holding for approximately three long seconds; (3) as you hold, sharply contracting the muscles in your stomach; (4) exhaling smoothly and easily. At the same time, relax the muscles in your stomach by mentally visualizing your stomach lining being coated with a soothing liquid layer. It may seem funny, but for the many people who suffer from stomach upset due to misdirected stress it is a great relief—instant, too.

Once you have swung the stress pendulum to a neutral position and the body is returned to a neutral state, you can think more clearly. Now you can decide how best to proceed. There are two positive positions on the stress pendulum, once it is out of negative. You must choose which of the two to aim for. It is important to note that each choice involves making a decision and doing something, even if it is deciding to do nothing. You may choose to negate the stress and take no more action.

It would be appropriate to decide to negate stress with no subsequent action when you are in an argument with someone you love. Imagine that you and your partner are carrying on a very casual conversation about a movie you both saw. The other person makes a statement about one of the actors with which you cannot agree. You begin to express your own opinion. At the same time you can feel the familiar reactions in your body surfacing.

Your lover refuses to listen to you. Instantly you feel your stress level continuing to climb. Smoothly and quickly you negate your stress reactions. Regaining your equilibrium, you see that your lover is still irate and it appears that no agreement is in sight. You assess the situation and decide that it is not important enough to pursue further. Carrying the argument any further would cause hard feelings and not contribute to what you want, a pleasant evening. At that point you decide that it is best to take no action and to simply drop the conversation.

The decision whether to take action or not after you negate your own stress will vary with each situation. Let's say that instead of arguing over a trivial matter, like a movie, the conversation between lovers was about a woman's earning a larger salary than her partner. The wife has recently been offered a job with a salary that is substantially larger than her husband's, and she needs to give the company an answer the next morning.

Even if the stress levels rose in this situation, it would be advisable to pursue the conversation. If the husband tried to end the conversation right away, it might be interpreted as an attempt to avoid the situation. Instead of lowering the stress level, it would add more stress. Throughout the conversation it is important that the couple continue to focus on what they want. At first, this may be work for them, and it does take time. But it is important to continue to focus on their wants. This helps to keep the pendulum in a positive position. Negative reactions are minimized and the conversation stays on the subject at hand.

It is important to remember that it takes an effort on your part to implement this process. One client in a Creative Relaxation training session was the president of a company. He said that when he was having difficulty communicating with one of his managers, he thought about using the Creative Relaxation technique, but decided that he was too lazy and instead blew his top and became very dictatorial. It took him more than two weeks to mend all the damage. He later admitted that it had not been worth it.

Once a person has become aware of both the symptoms and the causes of stress he can channel stress positively (providing he is willing to exert the effort). For instance, consider the case of Bob, a successful business executive who once found himself in a situation that is commonly identified as being distressful. Bob left his office fifteen minutes late for an appointment. Glancing at his gas gauge, he discovered that it was almost at the empty mark. Seeing a service station, he decided to go ahead and fill his tank with gas, even though the process would use up valuable time and was something he disliked having to do. As he turned his car into the station, he found that he was one of several drivers waiting in line. Instantly his body reacted to the situation. He felt his chest tightening and heard the familiar gurgling, churning sounds in his stomach. The clock ticked away. His mind began to create images associating time with money. His feelings of frustration continued to increase as he sat in his car.

The first thing Bob did was eliminate or remove the symptoms that resulted from channeling stress poorly—in other words, he negated the effects of stress. In his case it meant eliminating the tightening in his chest and the grinding in his stomach by following the steps for negating stress in specific areas. At that point, Bob decided that it would be smart to stay in line and fill his car with gas. Rather than wait nervously in his car, Bob decided to phone the man he was to meet, to say that he would be even later. Next, when he got back in his car, he decided to arrange the items of the meeting on an agenda, listing the most important ones first.

Another common stressful situation is having to wait in line, especially when you are traveling. Perhaps there are only a few minutes left to catch the last flight of the day and only one ticket agent is on duty. Even though you are next in line, the gentleman in front of you has a stack of tickets and appears to be having a problem. His problem could be the result of many things, but for you it means trying not to blow your cool.

If this is a common difficulty for you, you might try the following things the next time you find yourself waiting in line. First, ask yourself if it is absolutely necessary for you to wait in line. If so, immediately negate or neutralize any of the physical symptoms of negatively channeled stress. Many people have also found it helpful if they say to themselves, "Cool it," or "Relax."

You might also become aware of your thoughts. If you are thinking stress-building thoughts, try to think of your negative thoughts as negative tape recordings. Simply visualize in your mind turning off or cutting the negative tapes.

Another way to eliminate thinking negative thoughts is to replace the negative thought with a stronger positive thought. Some people have been successful in stopping the negative thoughts by actually talking out loud. You might also try asking yourself if your negative self-talk is an exaggeration. If what you are saying to yourself is not accurate, modify it.

If you have decided there is nothing you can do about the situation, figure out a way to use the time constructively. One busy professional woman spends her time in the supermarket line reading popular magazines. When her food is ready to be checked out, she calmly walks over to the magazine stand and returns the copy. Another shopper plans her meals for the week while she is waiting in the line.

Many of the techniques suggested in this chapter are the result of learning effectively to integrate Creative Relaxation into your busy day. The Pendulum Concept of stress is a simple process that can help you channel stress more positively during stressful situations. As we have seen, in order to gain maximum benefit from Creative Relaxation, you need (1) to know what it is you want, (2) to become aware of specific reactions, (3) to identify the cause or stressor, (4) to determine if your reactions are helping you to reach what you want, (5) to decide if you can eliminate or remove the stressor, and, if not, (6) either to negate the stress with no subsequent actions or to negate the stress with further action to attain your goals.

Sometimes even after a stressful situation has passed, we hold on to many of our stress reactions. These "ghost" reactions can occur knowingly or unknowingly. They serve no purpose, except to add more wear and tear on our bodies and to waste our supplies of adaptive energy. The stress reactions that haunt us after the stressor is gone are called the Stress Momentum.

The next chapter explains what the Stress Momentum is and how Creative Relaxation can get rid of it.

4 ✻ Your
Hidden Stress

It is common to find that when a stressor is removed, we continue to react as if the stressor were present. This is a needless addition to our daily stress level. Functioning at this higher stress level causes additional wear and tear on the body and wastefully consumes our adaptive energy supply.

The specific kinds of behavior that develop are usually not consciously observed. A typical example of unconsciously channeling stress can be seen when you have a passenger in your car who is not comfortable with the way you drive, and he keeps putting his foot to the floor on an imaginary brake. Another example is a person who fiddles with a paper clip, pencil, or rubber band throughout a meeting.

The Stress Momentum is defined as habitual stress-related actions that recur with no identifiable cause. The primary symptom of the Stress Momentum is a generalized feeling of uptightness or tenseness. Take, for example, Saul, who lived through a period of time when money was scarce. He learned to worry about not always having enough money to pay the family's bills. The hard times for Saul have passed and his income is plentiful. However, he continues to worry over even the smallest money matters.

Fran is another person who continues to have a reaction that does not serve any purpose. For years she worked for a boss who was difficult to get along with. In order to avoid getting into arguments, Fran learned to bite her lower lip. This helped her to keep her mouth closed and to not say something that she would later regret. Now, Fran works for a new boss. They communicate easily with each other. Yet she continues to bite her lower lip and has chapped lips in the winter as a result.

In either situation, to stop the Stress Momentum it is necessary to become conscious of your reactions. Next, you need to stop and undo your old reactions. In Saul's case, he has come to realize that his worrying has nothing to do with making or holding on to money. If he becomes aware that he is worrying about money, he stops and asks himself if his worrying is helping to resolve money matters. If it isn't, he lets go of these negative thoughts as he does when he practices the Personal Quiet Time.

Fran, on the other hand, has learned to stop the Stress Momentum of biting her lower lip by practicing the following: (1) she stops what she is doing, (2) she negates her stress by inhaling and exhaling smoothly, and (3) she listens to her boss with her lower and upper teeth touching one another. Sometimes she finds that sucking on a breath mint or a piece of hard candy helps her to stop the old habit of biting her lower lip.

No one should feel ridiculous for being caught in Stress Momentum. Here is how it starts.

The first stage in the process is unavoidable. A person

will learn several stress reactions to help him or her adjust to a real stressor. In the second stage, the person selects the most effective reactions to the particular stressor and continues to repeat them over a prolonged period of time. However, when the stressor is eliminated, the person continues the same reactions. The reactions, at this third stage, are habitual and unconscious.

Some common observable habitual stress reactions are cracking the knuckles, "motoring" the foot, rubbing the hands over the thighs, frequently scratching the head or forehead, rapidly blinking the eyes, twirling a lock of hair with a finger, licking the lips, picking or biting the nails, whistling or making other sounds with the lips or tongue, wiggling the toes, and eating without stopping. Other less obvious reactions are worrying, sitting on the edge of a chair or couch, constantly shifting one's position when sitting, jerky movements, frequent sighing, and pacing the floor.

When stress reactions are continuously produced, the person's adaptive body mechanisms "idle" at a higher stress level. Expected continuous stressors can be easily handled. But when an unexpected stressor arises, the person gets more easily upset and can overreact. One woman's gum chewing exemplifies how producing a habitual reaction continues to perpetuate uptight feelings. She discovered that whenever she felt uptight because of an uncomfortable situation, she craved chewing gum. Rather than feeling more relaxed when chewing the gum, she continued to feel anxious. The uptight feeling lingered as long as she continued to chew the gum.

Many people have learned to associate stress reactions like worry, pressure, anxiety, and fear with success. Such people operate at a high stress level. This often causes them to overreact to new stimuli or to be more irritable than usual. High stress levels can magnify nuisances and make them appear more serious than normal. They can spill over and "deposit" stress on other people. For example, one wife easily detects when her husband is having problems at work. John will come home at night and get irritated over things that generally do not bother him. When one of the children merely starts changing the television station during a show, John gets upset and angry.

High stress levels can also make people more sensitive to noise. John's wife has also learned to detect when John is more sensitive to noise levels. Instead of politely asking his son to lower the television volume, John growls and yells at anyone within range. His wife is pretty accurate at determining the severity of the problem by comparing it with the intensity of his growl. Her husband is communicating his high stress level. He is also adding to the stress levels of other family members. This pattern will continue unless he learns to identify his stressors and manage his anger. When the stress reactions inside our bodies are allowed to build without being released, the smallest stimulus can cause an explosion. For example, a wife may make an extra effort to please her husband for dinner by asking him what he wants to eat. Instead of interpreting his wife's request as thoughtful, the husband gets upset over her inability to make decisions. The explosion expands as he begins to point out numerous past incidents in which his wife had difficulty making decisions. Meanwhile, the wife is shocked and confused. She wonders how all this came about.

Another example of repressing stress concerns a young couple who initially enjoyed teasing each other. At first they were both laughing and finding each other's jokes very humorous. However, after a period of time the wife no longer found her husband's jokes so funny because they were loaded with double meanings. Each time he joked about her, she would store the negative feelings that were produced.

One day he made a comment about her rubbery pancakes. Instead of laughing, as he expected, his wife got extremely angry. She yelled at him about the joke and about his wit in general, and then questioned his intelligence. By the time she finished yelling she had introduced five other things about him that she was dissatisfied with. In this case the body's adaptive mechanisms are overworked and adaptive energy is needlessly wasted.

People learn to stop the Stress Momentum and rechannel their adaptive energy in more positive ways by first consciously recognizing their own habitual stress reactions. Next, before they can let go of the old reaction, they stop whatever they are doing. Once the momentum has lost its force, the person can replace the old reaction with a new, more desirable response to stress. For example, it was pointed out to one Creative Relaxation client that he always brought his hands together and fiddled with his fingers during a conversation. In order to stop the Stress Momentum, he separated his hands and deliberately placed them flat on his lap or across the chair arm. Each time he caught himself fiddling, he calmly undid his habit and went on.

Another client could not stop eating once she started. She found she could break the momentum by first recognizing the feeling that accompanied the urge to eat. As soon as she became consciously aware of her uncontrollable desire to eat, she immediately stopped eating, closed her mouth, and put all her eating utensils down on the table. As soon as the momentum stopped, the craving for food diminished and she was easily able to regain control of her actions.

One client perpetuated the Stress Momentum by frequently removing his glasses from his face and playing with them when he was talking to another person. Once it was pointed out to him, he was amazed to discover the number of times he did it throughout the day. He broke the momentum by stopping. Instead of taking his glasses off his face, he kept his hands in his lap or on top of a table.

If you perpetuate the Stress Momentum by "motoring" your foot, when you sit, try to stop the motion immediately and then practice placing your feet flat on the floor. Whenever you feel the urge to start motoring your foot, counteract the urge by relaxing the muscles in your lower leg and foot.

People have noticed the Stress Momentum slowing down almost immediately after stopping the reaction. They have described the change as a feeling of inner calmness. One client used the simile of a choppy lake that suddenly becomes calm and still after a storm.

You now have the skills for positively channeling stress. When someone suggests to you that you need to relax, and you agree, you do not need to ask yourself how to do it. The "how" is Creative Relaxation, which encompasses practicing the Personal Quiet Time and using the Pendulum Concept and the Stress Momentum to help you maximally benefit from using the technique during the day.

Positively channeling stress begins with you. As one client said, "By learning to channel my stress better, I will have more to contribute to others." The next chapter talks about you and shows you some ways that you can use Creative Relaxation to begin positively channeling your stress.

5 ❊ Turning Your Stress into Positive Energy

Many of life's stressors are out of your control. One familiar stressor occurs when you drive to work on the freeway in the morning and the traffic is congested. Finally, your car comes to a dead stop. Helplessly, you sit there knowing with each passing minute that you are going to be late. Another stressor occurs when you phone someone and he puts you on hold and then forgets about you. Another arises when your scheduled appointment arrives thirty minutes late without calling or apologizing.

Even though many of life's situations are out of your control, you do have control over how you choose to react. Our reactions can lead us either closer to or farther away from our goals.

Reactions that do not lead you closer to your goals are negative responses to stress. When you direct stress in negative ways you work against yourself.

You are working against yourself when you can't fall asleep the night before an important presentation. You work against yourself by calling yourself stupid and dumb when you spill your coffee right before you are going to a meeting at which you expect to be accurate and alert. Skipping meals and then later questioning why you feel so shaky and irritable is another example of using stress negatively.

These reactions can be costly to our health and overall well-being because they wastefully drain more of our adaptive energy supply. They are costly in another way in that they cause us to be less productive, efficient, and effective.

Learning to react in ways that will lead you closer to your goals is using stress positively. It is also learning how to be on your own team. When the game strategy of life is not unfolding as you planned, being on your own team means staying in there and continuing to react in positive ways.

There are two important things that you need to know in order to best work with yourself: (1) what you want and (2) how to listen to the signals that your body sends you.

Daily practicing of the Personal Quiet Time assists you in each of these areas. It can help you by giving you a daily stress reading. For instance, if you feel tired after practicing the PQT, your body is letting you know that you are driving yourself too hard. You have gone beyond your bounce-back capacity. I would suggest that you review your schedule for the last three days or ask yourself if something is bothering you. Then give yourself a time-out and rest.

If at other times you feel like jumping up and starting to work on various projects before your PQT is over, your body is signaling you that you are overstressed. That is all the more reason for staying there and finishing your Personal Quiet Time.

The PQT helps you to slow down and get to know yourself better. Many people have described it as a time when you can pull yourself off the merry-go-round of life and comfortably take an inventory of yourself. Goals are more clearly visualized. It is important that you invest some time to figure out what you want. Goal setting is a continual process. Once you know what it is you want, you need to build a ladder made up of tiny steps, each one building toward your goal. As an Eastern philosopher once said, a journey of a thousand miles begins with a single step.

However, it is important in goal setting to realize that always taking the toughest job first is not the most efficient way to begin. You do not climb a ladder by trying to jump to the top rung. You start with the bottom step and progress upward. To achieve goals, you must start with the first step in the sequence of building the whole.

Don't trust your memory. The first rung in the goal-setting ladder involves using a pen and paper. The following steps are helpful in writing down your goals:

1. Write the goals in the first person and choose goals that will help you be the person you want to be.
2. Write the goals clearly and concisely.
3. Write the goals in the present tense or as if you have already achieved them.
4. Write goals for all aspects of your life, including social, religious, professional, and financial life, marriage, family, leisure activities, hobbies, health practices, and recreational pastimes.
5. Write your goals as specifically as possible so you'll recognize them when you reach them.
6. As soon as you see yourself reaching a goal, establish a new one.

These goals can be short-term ones, dealing with immediate life situations. They can also be long-term, dealing with your lifelong aspirations. Once you've identified and defined your goals, begin to direct all your energies toward achieving them. When stressors interrupt your plans, you can, through Creative Relaxation, make use of your stress responses in helpful—not distressful—ways.

Many goals can be disrupted by interpersonal arguments. When you are arguing with another person, it is very difficult to calm that person down unless you can calm yourself down first. To regain your neutral stress balance, you first need to become aware of your own reactions. For example, check to see if you tighten the muscles in your chest and face or develop a knot in your stomach. Become aware of the tone of your voice. Notice if you speak more quickly or if you enunciate each word very distinctly, as if you were throwing a dart at the other person.

As soon as you begin to recognize familiar stress reactions, stop talking. Negate the stress reactions by inhaling fully and deeply. Hold for approximately three counts. Exhale very smoothly and evenly and at the same time negate the stress reactions by relaxing each of the muscles in your body, starting at your head and ending with your feet. As you are exhaling, ask yourself if you *really* listened to what the person was *meaning* to say. Remember that words are symbols for intentions. Communication experts contend that only 7 percent of a message being communicated is in the words used. Refocus on the main idea of the argument. Ask yourself what you really want to achieve as a result of this argument. At this point many people doubt that there is enough time to think and do everything that is suggested, but there is. Research experts such as Dr. Nichols have estimated that a person thinks approximately 500 words per minute. During a normal conversation a person speaks about 125 words per minute. A person listens to a speaker on the average for only ten seconds out of every minute. The extra time could easily be used to regain one's stress balance and refocus on the goals of the conversation.

As soon as you have considered these questions, before you speak, regain the relaxed feeling. Then speak very calmly and slowly. It's often helpful to begin the discussion by rephrasing what the other person last said. One way you might do so is by saying, "Am I correct in assuming that . . ." or "If I understand you correctly, you are saying that . . ." and then, in your own words, stating the point the other person was trying to communicate. Keep your goals in mind at all times.

Many personal goals involve building marital and family relationships. If you can't unwind and switch gears at the end of a working day, you can't contribute totally to building a family life. Many people tell me that they used to relax at the end of a working day by taking a drink. One executive came to see me because he was concerned about his growing need to have a few drinks each night to help him unwind. He wanted to learn how to unwind without alcohol. The corporate officers were impressed with his abilities and were quickly advancing him up the corporate ladder. However, the more responsibility he had, the more trouble he had unwinding and the more worried he became. Another concern that he and several of his colleagues expressed was the fear of dying from a heart attack at a young age because of all the pressures.

After three weeks of training in Creative Relaxation, this executive has learned to let the pressures go by practicing the Personal Quiet Time for fifteen minutes before leaving the office at the end of the day. He has also learned to maintain the relaxed feelings that resulted from experiencing the Personal Quiet Time as he drives home at night. He plays soft, relaxing music on the radio. As he drives, he mentally concentrates on regaining the relaxed feeling in each of the muscles in his body. Now, when he drinks, it's for fun and to be social, not to unwind.

In addition to relaxing all the muscles in the body, other people have found it helpful to review what everyone else in their family was doing on a particular day. As they mentally review each family member's daily agenda, they form questions that they want to ask each person when he or she arrives home. This mental activity accomplishes two things: (1) it helps a person more easily channel his or her thoughts away from the office; and (2) it helps to orient the person to the type of day everyone else has had, and this aids him or her in knowing how better to relate to others.

Practicing the PQT daily recaptures for many people the feelings that accompany a vacation. One client noticed that before learning Creative Relaxation, she used to reach a point where a vacation became a necessity. She was burned out, and going to work another day seemed impossible. Vacations to her were recuperations. The first three or four days of her vacation were spent sleeping and resting. By the time she unwound and was beginning to enjoy herself, it was time to go back to work. After practicing Creative Relaxation, she no longer has the panicky feelings that used to peak right before her vacation. Now when she goes on vacation, instead of recuperating, she is ready to play and enjoy different experiences.

Sometimes your goals may not conform with those of your family and friends. You must constantly reevaluate your goals and ask yourself if you can reconcile your own needs with the needs of others. A woman who attended a workshop in Creative Relaxation in Arizona told me that she felt like a "drummer out of step." She was a former English teacher. When her husband received a big promotion in his company two years ago, she decided to give up teaching. Now she feels bored. Many of the other company wives, with whom she is expected to socialize, talk mainly about where they went on vacation that year or about the yachts that their husbands were buying. The whole social scene to her was very artificial. She commented that maybe a lot of the wives put on airs and played the social role because they felt it was helping their husbands' image with other associates and clients. She said that twenty years from now she didn't want to be false like those other women. She felt like a drummer out of step because she couldn't relate to these women as she felt she needed to.

After updating and reevaluating her goals, she decided that she would associate with the executive wives only at important company get-togethers. At these social functions, she was able to incorporate her preference not to talk about materialistic things with the other wives by asking them about their interests and by listening.

Remember, goals change over a lifetime. At one point in life a businessman wants nothing more than to sit down and spend an evening discussing stock options over a few drinks. Later in life, discussing experiences and having a relaxed conversation may be his goal. If the same friends cannot meet the changing needs, then a decision has to be made and a new circle of friends ought to be developed.

It is difficult to reach goals when you are not feeling your best. For many people a common problem that interferes with the ability to be effective is headaches. A tension headache can often be eliminated if you learn to recognize what you do to bring it about. One manager learned that his headaches were caused by putting the phone receiver on his shoulder when he talked on the phone to leave his hands free for writing. Often, phone conversations would last fifteen minutes. He never recognized the tightening in his shoulder and neck muscles until the end of the day when the pain was severe.

Once he became aware of the tightening in his neck and shoulder from talking on the phone, he became aware of other times in his day when he would contract those muscles—for example, when he talked to a supervisor with whom he didn't get along. After his Creative Relaxation training was completed, each time he felt the muscles tightening he could relax them by reflecting back to the Personal Quiet Time when his entire body felt relaxed. He imagined the tensions "seeping out" slowly from his neck area, like fine sand seeping out of an hourglass.

Another person recognized that some of his headaches were caused by tightening the muscles in his shoulders and neck when he wrote. He became aware that as he concentrated on the report material he was preparing, he would tighten the muscles in his neck and shoulders by pulling them forward and crouching protectively over his work, head pulled in like a turtle's and arms held tightly to his sides.

He learned to rechannel his stress in more productive ways by working for shorter periods of time and then taking a break. At first, he would set a timer to buzz every fifteen minutes to remind him first to check his posture at the end of the working period and then to take a short break. Another way he reminded himself to sit up properly was to place a metal hanger across his back underneath his clothes; whenever he became engrossed in his work and unconsciously drew his shoulders forward, he would feel the pressure from the hanger. Immediately he would neutralize the negative stress reactions and sit up straight, relaxing the muscles in his neck and shoulders. In a few weeks, he was able to relax his body as he wrote, and to his relief his headaches went away.

An upset stomach can also interfere with one's ability to function optimally. Some people consciously or unconsciously direct the stresses of the day or of an argument to their stomach area. This is my vulnerable spot. When I am not managing the stress around me very well, my stomach begins to gurgle and make rumbling sounds. If you have this problem too, the next time you hear those sounds, inhale and tighten the muscles in your abdomen as you learned in step 1 or 2 of the Personal Quiet Time. If you have high blood pressure or if you think you might be hypertense, remember to continue to breathe as you contract your abdominal muscles. Otherwise hold for about five seconds, then exhale slowly and relax the muscles.

Goals are more difficult to reach when your body is tired, especially when this is the result of not being able to fall asleep at night. The inability to fall asleep easily at night usually occurs when you need the sleep the most. Many people find it difficult to fall asleep the night before an important presentation to a large group of people, or when a problem has to be worked out either at the office or at home, or when they have been working late and their minds have been active.

The night seems endless when you can't fall asleep. One person said that each time he tries to fall asleep, a panicky feeling arises that makes falling asleep even more difficult. The panicky feeling often increases with thoughts about the need to get enough sleep that night because of the importance of the next day's activities. These anxious feelings are interpreted physically as you begin to move restlessly on your bed. After tossing around several times, you often get so frustrated that you open your eyes in disgust, pound your fist into the mattress, and grit your teeth.

If this is your problem, try using Creative Relaxation. The first thing to do is to stretch out on your bed, preferably on your back. Select a pleasant scene from your previous experience that you know is relaxing. Don't try to visualize a new scene at this time. Slowly picture yourself in the scene, taking time to sense the comfortable feelings you associate with it. Relax each of the muscle groups in your body, starting with your toes and progressing all the way to your face. If thoughts about not being able to fall asleep enter your mind or if you find yourself thinking about the next day's schedule, don't worry. Simply let the thought pass by focusing on the scene or the muscle group. Continue practicing the PQT technique until you fall asleep or all night, if necessary. You may feel comfortable knowing that people who have practiced this all night report that they get up the next morning feeling refreshed. They are able to function well throughout the day with only minimal discomfort. Creative Relaxation is not a substitute for sleep, but when you have a sleepless night it's nice to know that you won't spend the next morning feeling exhausted and unable to function.

Maintaining your optimal stress level under various conditions helps to ensure reaching goals. Direct confrontation is an example of one situation that easily raises one's stress level beyond the point of optimum efficiency. Confrontations occur when you are interviewing for a job position, when you are taking an oral examination in college, when your boss questions the content of a report you recently submitted, when you are arranging divorce procedures, or when your spouse wants to know why the bills are so high at the end of the month. In these situations, emotions are easily aroused. When discussions become too emotional, rational thinking and problem solving are minimized. Sometimes goals are sacrificed. Creative Relaxation enables you to maintain a balanced stress level.

When answering questions, two points to keep in mind are: (1) get a feeling for where the question might be leading you, and (2) organize your thoughts before you begin to speak. Take the time to do this, because it affords you the luxury of using Creative Relaxation and at the same time enables you to organize your thoughts.

There are several techniques that you can use to gain time. The first is repeating the question, in your own words, to the questioner. You might begin by saying, "If I understand you correctly, you are asking me . . ." And then restate the question. Or you might say, "Am I correct in assuming that . . . ?" This accomplishes two things. It shows the other person that you are listening and that you accurately heard the question. It also provides you with the additional time needed to use Creative Relaxation to counteract the negative stress reactions and to organize your thoughts. Additional time is gained if you remember to wait for the person to respond to your question.

If you do not understand the question or if you need more information, two techniques are helpful. The first involves rephrasing the question incorrectly after the person asks you the question. The usual outcome is that the person asking the question will usually go beyond merely repeating the question. Not only will you gain time, but you will also gain additional information about the question. Or you can simply say that you do not fully understand the question. You might say, "I'm not sure I understand the question. Would you mind repeating it, please?" Again, time and additional information are gained.

You can also ask the person simply to restate the question to gain additional time. As you begin to answer, you can regain your composure by repeating the question first. Pausing before you begin to answer the question is also helpful for organizing your thoughts. You might sip your coffee or change positions in your chair. At the end of your explanation you can also ask, "Did that answer your question?" or "Was the subject area adequately covered?" This is useful because it gives the other person an opportunity to state his or her evaluation of your response. If he says yes, it opens the conversation for a new topic.

Negating negative stress reactions using Creative Relaxation is easily integrated and practiced when you repeat the question in the various ways suggested. Inhale before you repeat the question. As you rephrase the question, slowly exhale and create a wave of a calm feeling throughout your body. At the same time, review in your mind the main point you want to present and the substantiating facts needed to support your main point.

Generalizations about behavior and personality often cause us to react in inefficient ways. The common reaction is to become defensive. Always defending our reactions does not lead us closer to our goals. Integrating Creative Relaxation with the following suggestions can help eliminate reacting in defensive ways.

The first two things to do are familiar to you by now: (1) Listen to what you are saying. (2) Become aware of your physical reactions. If you find that you are justifying your actions or making excuses for your behavior, stop what you are saying. Next, negate the negative stress reactions that have accumulated. At the same time, ask the person if the purpose of this conversation is for you to defend yourself. Asking this question is helpful because it keeps the main idea of the conversation or meeting in the forefront. It also helps to avoid letting the conversation turn into a personal attack.

When a person makes a generalization about your behavior, it is also important that you get the person to talk to you in specifics. For example, let's say that your spouse tells you that you are always late. Rather than becoming argumentative or defensive, calmly ask, "What have I done recently that leads you to believe that I am always late?"

This helps to clarify the problem at hand and avoids aggravating it. Your overall benefit is that it helps you more easily to maintain your optimal stress level.

In some instances, we create conditions that make it difficult for us to maintain our optimal stress level. Sometimes we let ourselves get so overworked that we cannot concentrate effectively on one task at a time. This condition is usually created when someone overextends himself or makes a habit of putting off work. People attach many labels to this condition. One woman defines it as "hollow minutes," or lack of productivity. Another person labels it "making a lot of smoke, and going nowhere."

If you find yourself having difficulty concentrating on the task at hand, you might try practicing the following:

1. Stop whatever you are doing.
2. Negate the negative stress reactions as described earlier. At the same time, remind yourself that your conscious mind can think only one thought at a time, even though you can do several things at once.
3. Begin again, taking one step at a time.

Some techniques that people have found effective in helping them to minimize the pressured, overworked feeling include the following:

1. When paperwork seems insurmountable, try clearing off the top of your desk. Neatly place all of the papers and business items in a desk drawer. Remove one business paper at a time from your desk drawer. Complete what is necessary before dipping your hand back into the desk drawer. The manager of a tool company found that with this technique he seemed to accomplish more in a day.

2. Make a list of all the tasks you want to accomplish in a day. The list should be made the night before so that it serves as a guide for the next day. List the tasks in order of importance. Or you might grade the importance of each task with an A, B, or C. An A rating means that it needs to be completed that day. A B rating means that it should be completed today, but it can wait until tomorrow. A C rating means that it needs to be completed sometime in the near future and it's a bonus if you can complete it now.

Completing a task once it is started can be an effective way to lessen the stress of work. Bill, an office manager, prefers to work this way. He finds that this principle is most effective when he opens his mail. Before using this technique, Bill used to open up a letter, study it, and then place it in his drawer or on top of his desk with the intention of getting back to it later. He did that with the other mail he received. By the end of the day his desk was cluttered with papers that he needed to get to. Many nights Bill went home exhausted and discouraged because he felt he had accomplished nothing.

Now Bill simply takes one letter at a time and follows all the necessary steps until either the letter is in the trash or a reply is in a stamped envelope. He likes this approach because he feels that he accomplishes more in a day.

Sam is an executive who finds that practicing this method is not always the most efficient way for him to work. He said that some of his mail does not lend itself to an immediate decision. Rather than pressure himself to make an immediate decision, he has modified the "completing the task" principle to meet his needs by combining it with the daily list sheet. He merely selects the day when the decision should be reached and writes it down on that day's list sheet. This benefits Sam in two ways. First, it gives him enough time to think through the situation, and second, it ensures the completion of the tasks.

Some people feel tense about getting a job completed. One client said that she is usually enthusiastic at the start of a project. However, about three-fourths of the way through, boredom sets in and the flame of enthusiasm gradually burns out. Guilt enters her mind when she considers not completing the task. Invariably she continues to push herself, fighting herself the whole way just to get the project done.

Some people are satisfied to push themselves until a project is completed. Others look for less stressful ways. If you want a more comfortable way to get projects completed, you might try the following approach:

1. Decide whether the task can be broken down into parts or steps.
2. Break the project up into several steps. If possible, the steps should serve as stopping points.
3. Decide the date and time when the project is expected to be completed.
4. Decide which of the steps you are in the mood to complete first. In certain kinds of projects, some people choose to complete the hardest step first, in order to get it out of the way.
5. Take action.
6. If you get bored or tired, stop at the end of the step you are working on and go off and do another task, eat, or enjoy a break.

Vacuuming the house is a common task that easily lends itself to this approach. It can easily be completed in steps.

One woman divided the vacuuming into three sections. She decided that she would be satisfied if the weekly vacuuming was completed by Sunday afternoon.

The best time for her to do her heavy housework was on the weekends. Usually she would begin the Saturday household chores with vacuuming. She would vacuum one section of the house at a time. If she got tired or bored before the house was completely finished, she would give herself permission to stop and do something else. She easily put aside the vacuum in one of three convenient places in the house. This made it easy for her to begin working on the project again. In the past when she got tired, she would continue to drive herself just to get the project done. By always forcing herself to complete the job, she was beginning to dislike a task that she originally did not mind. She learned that the important thing is getting the vacuuming done by Sunday afternoon. Driving yourself and getting frustrated are not necessary to ensure successfully obtaining a goal.

There are times when a person feels uptight for no apparent reason. One person said that it is as if everything that needs to be done gets all intertwined. He didn't know where to begin. Remaining in this state interferes with one's ability to function optimally and makes reaching goals more difficult. If you find yourself feeling uptight and don't know which direction to turn, you might try practicing the following four steps:

First, and most important, stop what you are doing. It means putting your pencil down on the desk if you're writing, or walking out of the kitchen if you're washing dishes. Sit down and close your eyes. Negate the negative stress reactions by inhaling deeply and then fully exhaling. At the same time, relax your body, starting at your head and continuing down to your feet. Breathe deeply again, relaxing the body.

Next, get a sheet of paper and a pencil or pen and make out a list of all the things that need to be done that day. Estimate the amount of time needed to complete each project. Choose from your list the most important items that can be completed within the remaining time.

Many people have found that this process stops the feeling of being rushed. It can also help you determine how well you organize your time. Guilt feelings are eliminated because you can clearly see what really needs to be done instead of what you may have fabricated in your mind.

Another stressful condition that we ourselves create is playing the game called "Beat the Clock." The game is played by trying to squeeze extra tasks into a short amount of time. Players of the game have described it as "trying to cram a lot into a short amount of time, or leaving things until the last minute." The outcome of playing Beat the Clock is becoming overstressed, being late for activities or appointments, or causing arguments.

Charlie was a strong advocate of this game. At work he played the game by waiting until the last minute to write a report. There were occasions when it looked as if the clock was going to beat him, such as the time he had to present a report at a two o'clock meeting for one of his company's biggest clients. Throughout the morning he conveniently found other "necessary" tasks to complete. At twelve-thirty in the afternoon he suddenly panicked because of the realization that he had very little time left to complete the report. At one o'clock he buzzed for his secretary. Frantically, he handed her a six-page report. He labeled it top priority and told her that he needed it immediately. In his last breath he cunningly reminded his secretary that this client was one of the company's biggest customers. Charlie's increased stress was transferred to his secretary in the form of resentment. Her feeling of pressure mounted as she realized her time to complete the report was limited. Nervously she sat down at her typewriter and began typing the report, making more errors than usual.

As a result of going through the Creative Relaxation training, Charlie decided to continue to play the game, but under a new set of rules. Here are his revised rules:

1. He confines the game playing to himself.
2. In order to ensure winning at his own game, he gives himself extra time to get those extra things done.
3. He prioritizes all the things that he is trying to squeeze in.

In case his game strategy does not turn out as expected, or if his stress level gets too high, he can easily switch gears and stop the game without losing sight of his original objectives. He is not the only winner in this new game strategy— the other people who work with him also benefit from his winning.

Learning to calm yourself down and function more effectively during more stressful times is important. Learning to relax and work effectively with others is just as important. The next chapter discusses how.

6 ✳ You, Stress, and Other People

We have already seen that learning to lower your own stress level is important in helping you to deal with stressful situations. In your relationships with others, it is just as important that you act to keep their stress at a minimal level.

People frequently say that it is easier to channel stress positively "over things" than it is with people. Lawrence Galton, author of *The Silent Disease: Hypertension*, says that the greatest cause of emotional disturbance is other people. Often we knowingly or unknowingly increase the stress levels in others. One of the most common ways we do this is by dumping the frustrations of the day on others. Some people call this making others feel the way you feel. It's the old adage "Misery loves company." Unfortunately, we usually end up dumping our frustrations on the people we care about the most.

Many people are finding relief from this kind of syndrome. They are using the increased awareness of their body's stress level that they have gained from Creative Relaxation to help them give an accurate "Stress Report."

One of the most valuable times to use this Stress Report is at the end of the day when everyone comes home. Families are putting up stress boards in a visible area in their house. Each person tacks up a piece of colored paper on the board when he or she gets home to indicate his or her Stress Report. For example, in one family the color blue means that everything is "cool" and flowing well. Orange indicates that the person is feeling a little on edge from the day. That's a signal for others to not push. The color red means that the person is in a bad mood and is ready to dump his stress on the nearest victim. Other family members know to tread lightly. Feelings of being down or needing attention are indicated by yellow. Families like this reporting system because at a quick glance they can get a reading of how everyone really feels. A lot of arguments and fights are eliminated this way.

Another reporting system that people use is to ask each other directly, "What's this evening's Stress Report?" This question gives both people an opportunity to share how they feel. The benefits are the same as those of the Stress Report board.

If you know you are feeling extremely upset, before the other person makes the first move, warn him first about your present condition. Remind the person that your bad mood or increased stress level has nothing to do with him and that he should be understanding. It is also recommended that you highlight at that point some of the ways the other person can help you. Remember to phrase your points positively. For example, you can help the non-stressed person to help you by asking him to keep his conversation to a minimum, rather than saying, "Don't talk to me now." The last thing you want to do is add more stress to yourself and to those around you.

One of the most common communication problems with close relationships—especially with husbands and wives—is that guidelines on how to communicate effectively have not been established.

In business and even in games such as gin, backgammon, and golf, we are given various rules to follow before we begin to play the game. Yet in intimate relationships few people ever compare notes on the rules they think apply. Here are a few suggested guidelines that are essential to good communication.

A basic rule to follow in good communication is to stay on one subject at a time. It is not uncommon during an argument to lose sight of the original subject you were talking about.

People trained in Creative Relaxation have found that they become more aware of topic changes during a conversation. Take, for example, Joe, a manager and a father of two children. Whenever he feels uncomfortable during a conversation, he immediately readjusts the way he is sitting so that his body is situated in the most relaxed position. Next, he negates any negative stress reactions by practicing the methods previously described in this book. He also finds it necessary to stop any movements, like shaking his foot or playing with a paper clip, that might perpetuate the Stress Momentum. If he recognizes that the other person is changing the subject, Joe calmly says, "I'm not ready to go on that course yet, I still feel uncomfortable with . . ." or "I still have a question about . . ." and names the original subject.

Another basic skill in communication is to let the other person finish talking before you begin. This skill needs to be practiced regularly so that it becomes a habit. When emotions become aroused, it is most difficult to refrain from interrupting the other person. If you do, I suggest that you admit that you interrupted the other person and apologize.

Once the person has expressed his ideas, it is good practice to rephrase what he has just said before you make any comments. This is helpful to practice when the conversation seems to be going nowhere. The conversation becomes repetitive and the persons involved get defensive. When a conversation is at this point it means that one or both parties feel that the other person is not *really* listening. Rephrasing what the person last said in your own words eliminates this. It also gives you additional time, as mentioned in Chapter 5, to organize your thoughts and to assess whether you are staying with the original subject being discussed.

Let's say that a conversation turns into an argument. Try following the steps that were suggested in the last chapter:

1. Become aware of how you are reacting. Have you changed the tone of your voice? Are you speaking more quickly? Have you assumed a sharp tone of voice? Become aware of the reactions taking place in your body.

2. As soon as you become aware of your negative reactions, stop talking.

3. Negate the negative reactions by relaxing the muscles in your body with smooth breathing. At the same time ask yourself these two important questions:

    a. What do I want from this conversation regarding both long- and short-term goals?

b. Did I hear what the person was *meaning* to say?

It is common to feel anxious and hurried at this stage of an argument. This hurried feeling is natural. Your body is ready to defend itself because your fight-or-flight mechanism is activated. Take your time.

4. Once you feel you have regained your equilibrium, the next step is to regain the relaxed feeling as you begin to speak very calmly and smoothly.

In addition to regaining their own balanced state by implementing the four steps, many people have found that they are able to help others lower their stress by saying, "Let's take a moment to relax." Another couple finds it effective to follow that statement with saying "Truce" to each other and holding hands for a brief moment.

Another communication skill that is frequently neglected in close relationships is listening. A common complaint is that one or both partners in a relationship feel that the other person doesn't listen. Take Richard, for example. He gets extremely upset with his wife because she never seems to listen to him whenever he has important things to discuss. She does two things that infuriate him: she continues to work in the kitchen while he is trying to talk to her, and she always has an answer for him before he has had a chance to finish what he wants to say. Their discussions frequently turn into arguments.

Richard's wife learned after going through the training program in Creative Relaxation that just hearing what someone says is not listening. It is important to act like a good listener. Acting like a good listener means giving others your full attention and visually demonstrating to them that you are in fact listening. Common visual signs include making facial expressions such as raising your eyebrows, using your eyes for expression, smiling or frowning, nodding your head, or saying things like "'yes" or "I see" to let the person know you are following what he is saying. It also means asking pertinent questions and trying to get to the core of the other person's thoughts. Richard's wife further learned that it is important to let a person complete his thoughts without interrupting him with a response. Giving a correct answer is not the point. The important thing is that responding too quickly leaves the other person feeling uncomfortable and less important. It seems as if their problems aren't significant enough and you are thereby suggesting any solution just to get the person out of your way.

It was also suggested to Richard that he select a better time to talk with his wife. Unconsciously, he would come home at night and storm right into the kitchen. Immediately he would start talking to her and demanding her attention without being aware that she was busy preparing dinner, which he liked to have ready when he got home.

Often we forget to consider the other person's work load, physical condition, or mental state when we choose to talk. A perfect example of this commonly happens on the telephone. Many times when you're excited about talking with a friend or business associate you unexpectedly discover that the other person does not share your enthusiasm. Such calls should often be placed again later when the person is more receptive. In this case, Richard and his wife decided that the best time to talk comfortably with each other was after the children were in bed.

An adequate amount of time was set aside to talk whenever there was something to discuss. They each learned that good communication is a team effort. Communication is most effective when each person is willing to discuss a subject. If in doubt, it is always best to find out by asking. You might ask if the person has the time to discuss what's on your mind. If there is not enough time to talk, make sure you establish another day and time to get together.

The team effort in communication also means that each person needs to take responsibility for making sure that the message being communicated is understood. The technique of rephrasing is helpful here. You can also check with the other person by asking him if he understands. It is important to make sure that you wait long enough for him to have a chance to ask himself whether there is anything that needs further clarification. Implementing these and other good communication techniques becomes more difficult as the stress level rises.

The next time you feel your stress level rising during a conversation, try positioning your body in your most relaxed position. This enables you to negate the accumulated stress and to minimize your urge to interrupt other people. Maintain the relaxed feeling when you speak. When you are the listener, maintain the relaxed feeling in your body as you continue to breathe smoothly and evenly.

Stress is also created when one sets unrealistic expectations for another person. In marriage, people assume that their partner really should behave in certain ways even though the other person has never demonstrated a willingness to do so.

You need to examine your own expectations for the people around you and ask yourself, "Are they realistic?" For instance, one woman learned after asking herself that question that she had unfair expectations of her recently retired husband. She was still working. Each night she would come home and notice her husband sitting in his favorite chair doing nothing. Quickly she would survey the house and each time it looked as if no housework had been done. She would get upset because she expected him to be as active as she was. She feared his inactivity, which revealed itself in weight gain and boredom. The boredom that her husband was experiencing in combination with his weight gain was damaging their relationship as well as his health. As a result of going through the Creative Relaxation program, this woman became aware of her husband's needs and realized that each person has his own optimal stress level. Some people enjoy a heavy pace and know that they can sustain it throughout their lives, while others cannot. Each type needs to know what he or she can endure.

After watching how pleased his wife had become with her increased sense of self-awareness, this retired man decided to go for training in Creative Relaxation to find out what all the excitement was about. He became aware that some of his need to sit was motivated by a reluctance to accept the drastic change that retirement brought to his life. By not doing anything, he sought to avoid involvement in a future he did not really want. Some of the annoyance that he caused his wife was also an unconscious attempt to share his misery because he was unable to communicate his fear of the future. The training in Creative Relaxation helped him accept and take full responsibility for his "new" future. He went on a diet and got into a physical conditioning program to get back into good shape. The renewed activity on his part, in turn, made his wife much happier.

There are times when people impose their own standards of excellence on another person. Susan is an example of a woman who learned that much of the stress in her life was caused by her husband's placing the same expectations on her that he did on himself. Her husband, Ted, was very successful in business and prided himself in gaining expertise in all the things he did. He always set very high standards for himself. Ted would also impose these same high standards on Susan.

She would get extremely upset, especially when she was criticized for unimportant things, such as a dented license plate. On one warm Saturday afternoon they both felt like washing their cars together. In the process Ted noticed that his wife's license plate was dented. He fussed about it and became overconcerned about the situation. He persisted in his questioning her about it. In between asking her various questions, he fussed about having to fix it. Susan finally told him that the license plate was "no big deal." As soon as Ted heard that, he grew extremely upset. They got into an argument and each held his or her own ground. Two days later the incident was brought up during a Creative Relaxation training session. The couple reviewed the incident as an aid in helping them learn to identify the various kinds of stressors. The outcome of the discussion was positive.

Susan learned to understand her husband better, even after twenty-five years of marriage. She realized, with the aid of her husband, that it was natural for Ted to point out imperfections as he identified them. Pointing them out did not necessitate getting into a conversation. In most instances, the only feedback that Ted was interested in getting was acknowledgment. He told Susan that the reason he got upset was not so much that the license plate was dented as that she was lackadaisical about it. He said he would have felt better if she had merely said, "OK, it needs to be fixed." Susan has learned to profit from that incident. Now, whenever her husband points out something that isn't as it should be, she confidently says, "It will get fixed" or "OK, thank you for letting me know" or "OK, that's fine." Ted's verbal checking does not threaten her with immediate demands for action. An added benefit for both was learning to discuss certain uncomfortable incidences when they are both calm and not angry with each other.

In the case of Bill and Mary, expectations were, again, unrealistic. Over the years Bill has learned to discuss his problems. He believes that when a problem is shared it becomes half a problem. He feels frustrated because he expects Mary to deal with her problems in the same way. But Mary prefers to solve her problems alone. Bill and Mary learned that the way people adjust to stressful situations is different. What one person needs to help lower his stress level is not necessarily what the other person needs. Bill admitted that one of the reasons why he wanted Mary to talk out her problems was that he felt selfish for doing most of the talking and a little resentful that he needed her help with problems but she didn't need his. They both learned to accept and to work with each other's differences.

They integrated the Creative Relaxation technique to help them more easily overcome the uncomfortable feelings associated with changing their style of solving problems. Bill worked on repeating himself less often, and on limiting his explanations. Mary tried to speak more openly to Bill about some of her problems. As soon as they tried practicing this, they both felt a new sense of closeness. Mary became more aware that she needed other people. Bill acknowledged the special feeling inside that is associated with being needed.

Another source of interpersonal stress is found in the different ways people make decisions. One incompatible situation arises when a vague partner in the decision-making process is coupled with a decisive personality. The decisive person frequently gets infuriated and lacks patience with the weaker, less committal person. The natural impulse for the decisive person is to leave the indecisive person behind and plod ahead, making all the decisions alone. But that is not good for building relationships. Instead, the indecisive partner must learn to be methodical and concise in his approach to his partner. The case of Ann clearly illustrates the importance of learning how best to relate to the decisive type of personality. Before receiving training in Creative Relaxation, Ann would ask her husband vague questions. For example, if the bedroom needed redecorating, she would introduce the idea by saying, "Honey, I think the bedroom needs redecorating. Do you have any ideas?" She used this approach because she wanted to create an atmosphere in which they would both work together on the project. Even though her intentions were good, the end result was an argument after which each would walk away feeling frustrated.

Ann learned as a result of her training that her husband is a decisive person. The realization occurred when she considered that every day at work her husband was responsible for making decisions. Furthermore, her husband made his decisions on the basis of what types of alternative plans were available for consideration. In other words, he was not involved in assimilating the data. His expertise was in determining which among several approaches was most likely to lead the company closer to its goal.

At home, Ann expected him to get involved in planning the options in addition to making the final decisions. Her husband's frustrations grew from being involved with the planning stages, an area outside his expertise. Having gained this new awareness, Ann approached her husband with the idea of redecorating the bedroom by presenting him with several ideas from which to choose. Each option included pictures of the type of furniture desired, dates of delivery, paints and wallpaper samples, and total projected cost estimates.

When it's time to consider summer vacations, do not ask

your partner, "Where do you want to go this year?" Try, instead, to propose several specific alternatives, complete with itinerary, cost estimates, and proposed dates.

Another stress-producing situation arises when one person is designated as the excessive caretaker in a relationship. The existence of such a condition is commonly revealed with questions such as, "Where did we put our socks" or "We sure have a serious problem with . . ." or "Why did we do this?"

If you live with a person who routinely asks these questions, you may find over a prolonged period of time that your stress rises acutely. The first thing to do is negate your body's acute stress reactions by using the methods described earlier. Next, clarify in your mind the nature of the problem. Try to recollect, taking the time necessary to determine the immediate problem. Finally, locate who really has the problem. Once you have identified who has the problem, it is important that you do not let the other person's problem become yours.

One way you can do this is by verbally identifying or, if necessary, reclarifying the person with the problem. Let's say that Jim and Cindy are getting ready to go out for the evening. Jim yells for Cindy to come into the room where he is and asks where "they" left his shoes. Cindy reclarifies and properly identifies that George has the problem by calmly saying to him, "I don't know where you left your shoes last, I didn't see them, but I will help you find them."

If any insults or criticisms should result, remember not to take them personally. At the same time, don't stockpile stress. Handle each incident as it arises. Accumulated stress over time is dangerous, as we have seen.

Other people's lateness is a common stressor that frequently produces increased stress. It is much easier for you to accept your being late than it is to accept another person's lateness. Lateness of one partner in a marital relationship is a common occurrence. Frequently events that were initially planned to be enjoyed turn into disasters because of the arguments that couples get into over lateness.

If an enjoyable time together looks as if it might be sacrificed because you are getting upset over your spouse's lateness, try the following:

1. If the event is planned ahead of time, try refreshing your spouse's memory that day by writing a note and reminding him or her when to be ready to leave. Leave the reminder in a noticeable place so that your spouse can't give the excuse that you didn't tell him or her.

2. Sometimes it is helpful to check with your spouse to find out the reason why he or she is late. Before you permit yourself to get upset, ask your mate to clarify for you if he/she is being late purposefully to irritate you because of something you have recently done or if he/she is late for other reasons. Perhaps your estimate of the time you need to prepare for an evening is not realistic for your mate.

3. Instead of sitting and getting irritated, get involved in doing small projects that can easily be postponed as soon as your spouse announces he/she is ready. There is nothing worse than getting wrapped up in the game of "change-up," when one person finally gets ready and the one who was originally waiting is no longer ready.

In "change-up" both partners will scurry around and try to sneak in numerous last-minute tasks. If it is important to be on time, avoid getting into that kind of situation by choosing projects that can easily be dropped. One husband waits for his wife in their car and practices Creative Relaxation. He told me that it stops him from getting angry or annoyed with his wife. Besides not letting his wife upset him, he feels more refreshed and alert when they leave.

Another person uses this same technique during her working day. Whenever she goes to meet her husband, she carries reading materials with her. If he is late, rather than get upset as the clock ticks away, she merely uses the time constructively by reading.

If you are meeting people, you might take it upon yourself, as you wait, to call and notify them that you and your spouse are running late. This helps to lower their stress levels. Some couples have improved their "on time" record by indicating on the note a time to be ready that is fifteen or twenty minutes earlier than is necessary.

Many of the interpersonal stressors that add stress to everyone's life come from petty everyday irritants. For example, you and your spouse are putting away the groceries after going shopping. As you place the box of cookies in the pantry, your spouse insists that you put them on a particular shelf where they normally never go. When you ask why, the answer you get is "That is where they belong, that's why."

Another daily stress raiser appears when you and your spouse are about to get into your car. You start to clean the windshield but the windshield wipers don't work. For the next fifteen minutes you hear a long lecture on how dangerous it is for you to drive when your windshield wipers don't work. Thoroughly convinced, you offer to stop at the nearest gas station to get them fixed, but your spouse says, "No, not now."

Or you may be in a restaurant dying of thirst. You ask

one of the employees of the restaurant for a glass of water, but she tells you that her job is to serve butter.

Then there is the incident at work when someone tells you specifically to do one thing and then turns right around and asks you why you haven't completed another task.

It can be just as frustrating to be talking to a dissatisfied customer. Calmly you try to help him understand the situation by explaining the complaint process step by step. The whole time, he is agreeing with you. Then at the very end of the conversation the customer comes back at you with the same nonspecific complaint.

The examples are endless. In any case it is advisable to keep in mind what one woman learned: "It's not worth it to waste your adaptive energy supply on these kinds of situations." Creative Relaxation can teach you to let go and to go on.

7 ❋ Common Questions Asked about Creative Relaxation

Before learning how to apply the technique of Creative Relaxation to stressful situations in everyday life, you might want to review what you have read so far. The following questions and answers should help clarify any queries you may have. Also, at the end of this book, there is a brief summary of the steps involved in the PQT as well as suggestions for creating relaxing scenes, times, and places.

QUESTION: Is there a simple, generalized way to remember exactly what stress is?
ANSWER: Yes—think of stress as a reaction that your body makes to help you adjust to various situations.
QUESTION: Are tension and anxiety the same thing as stress?
ANSWER: No, but people use the words interchangeably. Tension and anxiety are examples of a stress reaction.

Tension refers to contractions of the muscles in your body.

Anxiety is a generalized fear reaction to some unspecific source.

QUESTION: If stress is a reaction, then what causes us to react?

ANSWER: A stressor. There are the stressors that arise in everyday situations that affect each of us in our immediate environment. The situations are unique to each person. The type of stressors that many of us overlook are those involving disease and accident. There are stressors of the natural life cycle (such as the frustrations of infantile dependency, the adolescent struggle for independence and identity, and the physical limitations of advancing age). Another type of stressor that directly affects the majority of the population comes from various "landmark" life events (the beginning of formal schooling, graduation from school, entering the job market, getting married, going on vacation, and getting a job promotion).

QUESTION: Channeling stress may be good, but isn't it better to avoid it altogether?

ANSWER: No. According to Dr. Hans Selye of the University of Montreal, stress is a natural reaction and is essential to living. The only time we are not reacting is when we are dead. As long as we are alive, we are under stress. Each of us needs to learn ways either to control stress or to re-channel it.

QUESTION: If stress is a natural response and not a disease, how can it be contagious?

ANSWER: When people are overstressed and don't know how to channel it constructively, they only channel stress destructively. Frequently the victims of this contagious stress are loved ones and co-workers. At times, an innocent bystander may even be placed under stress when near such a person.

QUESTION: Can anyone learn to practice the Creative Relaxation technique?

ANSWER: Yes. However, the challenge is not learning the technique, but continuing to practice it regularly and remembering to apply the training in everyday situations.

It is important to understand that the technique is designed for and is most effective with adults and adolescents. The program as described is not recommended for children, who have different needs.

QUESTION: How does Creative Relaxation differ from other relaxation techniques, such as Transcendental Meditation (TM)?

ANSWER: Creative Relaxation differs from TM in three ways. First, Creative Relaxation does not use a mantra as TM does. Both Creative Relaxation and TM allow the free flow of thought and involve letting go of thoughts, but in Creative Relaxation you do so by returning attention to the scene you're visualizing or to the muscles you're relaxing, whereas in TM you do this by returning to the mantra. Creative Relaxation uses a visual image while TM uses a sound.

One learns in Creative Relaxation how to let go of thoughts during the Personal Quiet Time and later is able to transfer this skill to everyday events (for instance, leaving work without taking unpleasant or worrisome thoughts from the day home with you).

Another way that Creative Relaxation differs from TM is that a person is not directed inward when practicing the Personal Quiet Time. With TM, one of the purposes of repeating a mantra is to help direct you inward until you reach the source of thought. The Personal Quiet Time is not designed to direct you inward. It is a vehicle to help you easily and enjoyably to become physically and emotionally relaxed and mentally refreshed by directing the mind "out-ward" toward the body.

The third way that Creative Relaxation differs from TM is that you can benefit from the technique during your busy day. In other words, you do not have to remove yourself from a stressful situation in order to benefit from using Creative Relaxation.

QUESTION: Is Creative Relaxation like Deep Muscle Relax-ation?

ANSWER: Just as TM focuses on directing thoughts in-ward, Deep Muscle Relaxation concentrates only on relax-ing the muscles in the body. The five Progressions in the Personal Quiet Time train you to relax physically, men-tally, and emotionally.

QUESTION: In general, what can I expect to feel after prac-ticing the Personal Quiet Time?

ANSWER: Many people notice that their thoughts have slowed down, they have an all-over calm feeling, and the muscles in their bodies feel relaxed. After a few minutes most people report feeling more alert and having more energy. Your feelings may naturally be different from those of others. The important thing is not that you feel the same as everyone else afterward, but that you feel better and function with more energy throughout the day.

QUESTION: Why is it important not to evaluate myself dur-ing the Personal Quiet Time?

ANSWER: The main reason is that your thoughts are not always consistent with what is actually happening in your body. For example, on the days when you exercise, have you ever felt that you were just too tired to exercise and wanted to put off exercising to another day? If instead of canceling out you do go to the track, the tennis or racquet-ball court, or the gym to work out, after a few minutes of activity you suddenly realize that your body is physically strong and that you are having an enjoyable workout. All the signs of tiredness have disappeared. The same kind of inconsistency can occur when you practice the Personal Quiet Time. You may feel that because your mind is active and thinking numerous thoughts, your body is not relaxing.

Another reason not to evaluate yourself during the fifteen- to twenty-minute period is that the effectiveness of the technique is determined by the improvements you notice during your active day. For instance, you may find that you need less sleep, or are less irritable, or are better able to handle uncomfortable situations. This is when the technique ought to be evaluated.

QUESTION: If I skip my PQT for a while, will I lose everything the training taught me?

ANSWER: No. Learning the PQT is like learning to ride a bike. Once you learn how, you can easily pick it up again. Even if you occasionally miss practicing, you can still benefit from using the PQT. As you will recall, Creative Relaxation is also practiced during your busy, active day when you are face to face with stressful situations. As one woman says, "The Personal Quiet Time is when I recharge my motor and get a bearing on where I am going." Using the technique during the day to channel stress better helps her to live more positively.

QUESTION: Sometimes it is hard for me to sit or lie down for the full twenty minutes when I practice the Personal Quiet Time. Is this unusual?

ANSWER: Not really. Rather than worrying about it and adding more stress, think of the feeling as a guide or message that your body is sending you. Most people have found that, when they feel like jumping up before the twenty-minute period is over, it is a sign that they are "uptight" and it is all the more reason why they should go on with the session. Many people have noticed that after a busy day, it sometimes takes about ten minutes before they begin to lose that hurried feeling.

QUESTION: Is it all right to practice the Personal Quiet Time without music?

ANSWER: When you are first learning the technique and going through each of the first three Progressions, it's better to practice the Personal Quiet Time with music. It is important, when personalizing the technique to meet your needs, that you decide how helpful music is in enabling you to relax. If you encounter a stressful situation, you want to be able to call upon the most effective aspects of the technique to help you deal with the situation. Knowing what aspects of the PQT are most beneficial to you is like knowing you have something to wear that is comfortable and complements you at the same time, when you have an important engagement to attend.

Once you reach the fourth Progression in learning the technique, then you are free to choose whether you want to use music or not.

If at any time during your training you find yourself saying that you will practice the Personal Quiet Time later because it takes too much energy to get the music ready, then immediately sit down and do the Personal Quiet Time without music.

QUESTION: Does it matter if I sit down or lie down to practice the Personal Quiet Time?

ANSWER: No. Choose whichever posture is more comfortable for you. If you tend to fall asleep when you lie down, then it is better to do the PQT sitting up.

QUESTION: Should I use an alarm clock to signal me when the twenty minutes are over?

ANSWER: If, at first, it helps you avoid being late for work or an important meeting, then go ahead and set the alarm. Be sure to give yourself some time to reorient yourself before jumping up to turn off the alarm. In order to judge the time, many people practice the PQT with a clock close by. During the twenty minutes people will periodically open their eyes to see when the session is over. One woman liked to set the timer on the oven to tell her when the twenty-minute period had passed.

QUESTION: Does it matter if I do the Personal Quiet Time only once a day?

ANSWER: Once a day is better than not doing it at all!

QUESTION: What if my spouse refuses to practice Creative Relaxation? Will the technique still benefit me?

ANSWER: Yes. The technique is individual.

QUESTION: Can I practice Creative Relaxation with other people around?

ANSWER: Yes. Even when you practice the PQT, you can have other people present. You may notice that it is easier to do the twenty-minute period alone. That is the ideal way to practice it, but it is not always the most practical way.

As you begin to integrate the technique into your busy day, you will find, as other people have, that it is most advantageous to practice the technique with other people around.

QUESTION: What if I can't find the time to practice the Personal Quiet Time?

ANSWER: Initially, you are not going to find the time. You must make it. Your day is already filled with things to do. Some people make the time by setting an appointment to practice the Personal Quiet Time, just as you would to see your doctor, dentist, or hairdresser. You need to develop the habit of practicing the PQT each day, just as you brush your teeth each morning when you get up.

QUESTION: Will people think it's strange if I go off by myself and practice the Personal Quiet Time?

ANSWER: Possibly, at first, there may be a few people who

are resistant to seeing you change. By practicing the PQT, you have changed their picture of you. However, with time, these few people will begin to reap benefits from the changes you have made—as when your boss sees that you get along better with others and have more energy throughout the day, or when your spouse notices that you fall asleep more easily at night. Then they will no longer question the value of your practicing the technique.

QUESTION: What is the shortest amount of time you recommend for practicing the Personal Quiet Time?

ANSWER: At least ten minutes. Research indicates that it takes approximately ten minutes for most of the changes to take place in your body in order for it to reach a hypometabolic state (a state of decreased metabolism). Even though several clients claim they feel more refreshed and calm after practicing the PQT for five minutes, I still recommend at least ten minutes.

QUESTION: Can I use the technique when I'm sick?

ANSWER: Yes.

QUESTION: Will it help me get better faster?

ANSWER: At this time there is no research to substantiate whether Creative Relaxation can help you recover more quickly from an illness. Several people claim they were able to shorten the amount of recovery time. Many others have found that practicing the technique when they are ill helps to minimize the discomforts. People who suffer from chronic illness have reported that practicing the PQT also helps to overcome the boredom that frequently accompanies it.

QUESTION: When I practice the Personal Quiet Time, do I need to tighten each of the muscles in the same sequence indicated in Chapter 2?

ANSWER: Only at first. The Personal Quiet Time of Creative Relaxation is just that—personal. Once you feel comfortable practicing the first three Progressions in Creative Relaxation as I have suggested, then feel free to vary the technique according to your needs, as Progression IV suggests. In order effectively to learn the skill of Creative Relaxation, it is important that at first you follow the suggestions with each of the Progressions. As soon as you feel comfortable with practicing each of the Progressions, it will be easier to vary the technique to suit your changing moods and needs. Remember, follow the guidelines for the Personal Quiet Time each time. It is not a question of doing something right or wrong when you practice the technique. Instead, focus on what is most comfortable and pleasing to you.

QUESTION: Can I still benefit from practicing the PQT if I have difficulty imagining a scene each time?

ANSWER: Yes. If you have difficulty imagining a scene each time you practice the PQT, and if it interferes with your relaxation, then for now do not attempt to place yourself in a luxurious scene. Instead, use the music to assist you as you mentally direct your attention to relaxing each of the muscle groups in your body. It is not necessary to imagine a scene vividly in order to benefit from the technique. The purpose of visualizing a scene is not to create a detailed picture of reality—it is to create a scene that enables you to relax more easily.

QUESTION: I don't like tightening my muscles to relax when I practice the Personal Quiet Time. Is it OK if I don't?

ANSWER: Yes. You should be pleased with yourself for recognizing those aspects of the Personal Quiet Time that are not as effective for you as the other components of the technique. Make sure you ask yourself why and then keep up the good work.

QUESTION: Can I switch scenes along the way if I feel like it?

ANSWER: Yes, as long as it feels comfortable to you during the PQT, and as long as you feel refreshed when you go back to your activities.

QUESTION: Sometimes I feel more tired after practicing the twenty-minute PQT. Am I doing something wrong?

ANSWER: No. Feeling more tired after practicing the Personal Quiet Time is your body's way of telling you that you are driving yourself too hard. Only by letting your body unwind do you discover that you have been pushing yourself too hard. Take a few minutes to review in your mind what you are doing each day and to ask yourself if anything is troubling you. You might try referring to the Pendulum Concept of stress to assist you in this situation.

QUESTION: When people are learning the PQT, is it uncommon to go through each of the muscle groups in the body in fewer than fifteen minutes?

ANSWER: No, it is not uncommon. If you find that you get finished ahead of time, try any or all of the following suggestions the next time you practice the technique:

1. Refer back to the scene more often.
2. When you contract the muscles, try holding for a slow count of three.
3. Take more time to feel the muscles relaxing.
4. Allow the music to help you relax each of the muscle groups before moving on to the next one.

QUESTION: Why is Creative Relaxation better than tranquilizers in dealing with stress?

ANSWER: Such drugs can be addictive. They may hide stress responses for a limited time, but they don't train you to channel stress so that you can prevent the situation from arising again. Drugs make you dependent, not independent.

QUESTION: Sometimes I find that I still go back to my old ways of mischanneling stress even after Creative Relaxation training. What am I doing wrong?

ANSWER: You are not doing anything wrong if you still respond to stress with the habits you have acquired over the years. It is unfair to expect yourself to make many changes after only a few weeks of Creative Relaxation training. It took you many years to develop certain habits, and you need to give yourself time to unlearn the old habits and relearn new ones. When you are trying to change, sometimes it is helpful along the way to recognize and reward yourself for the smaller changes that you are making, instead of waiting until you get to your final destination.

QUESTION: Would you review the basic guidelines that are essential to follow each time I practice the Personal Quiet Time?

ANSWER: There are five basic guidelines that you need to keep in mind:

1. Make your scene as idealistic and comfortable as you want.

2. During the PQT, do not make any associations with anyone or anything else. This is your opportunity to be alone with yourself.

3. Allow thoughts to enter and leave your mind very easily. It is not necessary for you to try to make your mind blank.

4. Do not worry if you feel that you are not relaxing a particular muscle well enough. There is no success or failure when you practice the Personal Quiet Time. You merely experience the technique.

5. Evaluate the technique when you go back to your busy day.

QUESTION: In the Pendulum Concept of stress, is it necessary to follow each of the steps in the exact order, in order to channel stress more positively?

ANSWER: No. However, when you feel confused, it might be helpful to sort out your thoughts by referring to each of the steps in sequence. Even though it is not necessary to follow each of the steps in the exact order in which they are given, it is important that you consider each of the steps, to help you channel stress more positively.

QUESTION: Is there something wrong with me if my goals change along the way?

ANSWER: No. It is important for you to keep in mind that goals are challenges that you set for yourself because you want them. You should try not to compete with your goals. Remember, you are the team, and goals help give your team direction.

QUESTION: Do people usually have such a hard time finding out what they really want?

ANSWER: Yes. Many people do not know how to determine realistically what they want. The second most difficult task is to figure out what you are going to do about your present situation, and the third, to gather your forces to take action.

QUESTION: Is it OK to get angry and yell after you've been through Creative Relaxation training?

ANSWER: We are not machines and we should not expect ourselves to act like machines. There may be times when you just feel like blowing it. When you do, you also need to be willing to pick up the pieces afterward.

QUESTION: Are you saying that we should do everything in life because we want to?

ANSWER: Not exactly. What I am saying is that the more things you do in life because you want to, the more fulfilled you will be, and the more effectively you will channel your stress.

QUESTION: If things are going great, do you still recommend that I practice Creative Relaxation?

ANSWER: Yes, absolutely. Remember, you are always experiencing stress. You still are reacting, even if you are getting the things you want.

QUESTION: Will Creative Relaxation automatically make me a better athlete?

ANSWER: No. You need to have the skills and the talent. Creative Relaxation doesn't make someone something he is not. By teaching you to channel stress better, the Creative Relaxation program enables you to perform your skills more easily.

QUESTION: Are you saying that exercise is not relaxation?

ANSWER: Yes. When you are relaxed, according to the scientific definition of relaxation, your body is at ease physically, mentally, emotionally, and chemically. Exercise does not ease the body. Exercise adds stress to the body. Both exercise and Creative Relaxation are essential in channeling stress positively and maintaining optimal health.

8 ✳ Turning Stress into Success in Business

The business of business is the production of goods and services at a profit. Any business is only as good as the team that operates it, the management that directs it, the people who carry out its functions, and the investors who back it. These people—managers, employees, and investors—are exposed to their own personal stresses and to stresses created by other people. In the relationships of these people, internal stress can arise from four sources: (1) from power relationships, (2) from insufficient information, (3) from competition against oneself and others, and (4) from personality conflicts. Added to the "in-house" stressors are the external stressors: (1) the international economic situation, (2) current banking practices, (3) stock market fluctuations, and (4) an unpredictable consumer market.

People in business are exposed to two types of stressful situations in which Creative Relaxation can be a tool for effective performance on the job. The first is the ongoing predictable job stressors. The problems that arise from one's job role and the demands of meeting deadlines fall into this category. The second type is the sudden crisis stressors that plague us unexpectedly.

The stressors that business people face are real. No one person is responsible for creating many of these internal and external stressors. Nevertheless, your responsibility to yourself is to learn how to cope with them effectively.

THE STRESS
OF MANAGEMENT

The manager, or boss, is responsible for making sure a company makes a profit and that all departments within an organization function efficiently and productively.

There are several kinds of bosses. One type of boss operates within a corporate structure. He is in charge of some personnel and, at the same time, reports to his supervisors. In this job role, he is in competition with his peers. Another type of boss is the person who owns his own business. Often the boss of his own company wears many hats and is open to multiple stressors.

Even though these bosses have different responsibilities, they have several stressors in common. One of the unique factors about the boss is that he has to solve his own problems. In order to identify his problem clearly, it is important that a boss learn how effectively to rechannel the anxieties and tensions that mount in a day so that he doesn't let them spill over to the next meeting, the next day, the next problem.

Take Mark, an executive for a large corporation. He discovered that on days when he had meetings back to back, if the first meeting went badly he would go into the next meeting with a "mad hangover." The anger and frustration created in the first meeting had a way of following him throughout the day in a snowball effect.

Another executive said, "It's like when you go to tie your shoes in the morning and the shoestring breaks, the whole day is a wipe-out." Mark realized that carrying these reactions of distress throughout the day was not desirable. This thought pattern would always seem to reach a dead end when he asked himself the question, "What do I do about this?" After going through the workshop in Creative Relaxation, he found that the technique helped him eliminate the mad hangover. He used the technique in the following way:

First, he learned to recognize the earliest symptoms of the mad hangover. He felt the muscles in his jaw and his chest tightening and he would nervously shake his right foot. Mentally, he would repeatedly replay those points of the meeting that were distressful. With each replay the feelings of anger and frustration would mount.

Once he could identify the typical signs of the mad hangover, he proceeded to negate the reactions. He found that the best way for him to rechannel the stress was physically and mentally to stop what he was doing. Next, he found it easiest to negate the physical reactions first by breathing deeply and smoothly. As he exhaled he pictured a former teacher of his who would speak to him with words of comfort as he proceeded to relax all the muscles in his body. He then began his own "self-talk." He usually would say to himself, "My energy supply is too valuable to waste like this." He would follow that statement with, "OK, I know I'm upset, but now is not the best time to think about it. I'll think about it later when I have the time to do something about my thoughts." He then would picture in his mind a tape recorder. He would record the thoughts on an imaginary cassette. Once he inserted the tape in the machine he would mentally see the thought leave his mind after the play button was pressed down. The mad hangover would be gone by the time he walked into his next meeting.

Another common stressor for bosses arises from the need to delegate responsibilities to others. Patience is an important survival skill that a boss needs to practice when delegating authority—and it's especially important when things don't go the way the boss expects. The boss has to deal with the fact that he often has little control over the situations created by his employees.

Losing the power to control is a tremendous stressor to a boss because his function and his expectations routinely involve controlling or directing others and making important decisions. When a boss encounters a problem situation in which he has limited his own authority, it is usually a test of his patience. For example, the boss may have to delegate the company's inventory to one of his employees because he is suddenly called out of town and is unable to complete it himself. When he returns, he expects to see the completed inventory. Instead, he discovers that the work was not done. The boss gets extremely upset and blows up at the employee without waiting to hear an explanation. The employee walks out of the office angry.

While the boss was away, one of the company's oldest clients sent in a big order that needed to be filled immediately. The employee temporarily in authority decided to fill the order first before doing the inventory. Later, the boss discovered all the details of what went on during his absence.

Creative Relaxation helped the boss avoid immediately overreacting to a situation. At the same time, the boss was more patient and was able to listen more. Creative Relaxation also helped him in this case to call the employee and apologize.

Take Warren, a top executive for a large textile company in Detroit. Over the past ten years his company has grown at a tremendous rate. The company now has five plants in three states. As a result, Warren spends much of his time traveling by plane.

Originally, Warren was interested in learning Creative Relaxation to help him unwind at the end of his routinely hectic day. But, as he mastered the techniques of the training program, he found that he was able to use Creative Relaxation during annoying travel delays, which call for patience.

One evening, his superior told him that the next morning he had to fly to Washington. His assignment was to chair an important planning meeting. Warren had only a few hours to prepare, and he was not looking forward to attending this meeting. The next morning at the airport he rushed through the baggage check-in line, and, fearful of being late, he ran all the way to the gate. The final call for his flight was being announced as he gave his ticket to the flight attendant. He was still out of breath as he took his seat and made ready for the plane to taxi out on the runway. Instead of preparing for take-off, the pilot announced on the loudspeaker that they had not been cleared for take-off and that it would be "just a few minutes."

For the first time, Warren noticed feelings of impatience. He was concerned because the meeting would start shortly after his plane was scheduled to land. He couldn't be late. His initial fear of being late for take-off was replaced by anxiety about being late for the meeting.

All during the flight he could imagine how the work back at the office was piling up on his desk. The feelings of urgency and frustration increased. The petty annoyances grew more irritating, and valuable time disappeared faster and faster.

Once in the air, the plane made up for the ground delay and Warren felt better. The pilot announced as they were approaching Washington that they would not be able to land because a smaller private plane was blocking the runway. The pilot predicted that they would be circling the airport for approximately thirty-five minutes. Warren again felt panicky. He felt his heart pounding and his chest tightening. The thought occurred to him to try practicing Creative Relaxation. He sat back in his seat, turned on the radio, selected a channel that played soothing, relaxing music, and practiced his Personal Quiet Time. When he was finished, he maintained his calm feeling by saying to himself that he had done everything he could. He admitted to himself that he didn't like the thought of being late, but neither getting upset nor indulging in drinking the free champagne that the flight attendants were handing out would help him to be effective at his meeting. An hour and a half later the plane landed and Warren walked off the plane sober and with self-assurance. He calmly greeted his colleagues.

When he related the incident later, he admitted that the way he acted was unusual for him. In the past he would normally have become upset and would arrive at the meeting angry and unable to think clearly. "This Creative Relaxation thing really works," he said.

The stresses of owning your own company are real and can be even more stressful than the stress of a life encapsuled in a large corporate structure. The boss in a small company often fills several roles out of the need to keep overhead costs down. Pressure is created when he tries to meet the demands of handling the business and making sure that his people are working optimally so that he sees a fair profit. As a result, small-business owners typically tend to worry more. They feel that when something goes wrong, they are the ones who end up eating the cost.

One of a boss's chronic worries is the loss of a top salesperson or an important employee. Bob was one small businessman who recently experienced the stress of losing his number-one salesman.

After Bob returned from a week's vacation, he decided that it would be a good time to get all his staff people together and organize the sales campaign for this season's new stock. He proceeded to call his top salesman first to see about setting up a date. To Bob's surprise, his salesman was in Vancouver, supposedly vacationing with his wife. Bob's mind instantly became flooded with fear. Thoughts raced around in his mind. His salesman had never mentioned a vacation to him.

Even though his relationship to his employees seemed smooth, Bob began to have doubts about his salesman's satisfaction with his job. Was the salesman looking for another position? Bob shuffled around the house all evening like an angry bear. He managed to tell his wife that he would be worried sick until his salesman returned home. His wife interpreted that to mean that he would be irritable and difficult to live with as long as he didn't know what was really happening.

Luckily for Bob, the period of intense worrying lasted only three hours. One call from his salesman reassured him completely. However, the energy that he wasted over that period of time produced nothing useful and will never be regained. It is interesting to note that by 10:30 P.M. the same evening, Bob's eyes were closed, because of "exhaustion." What would have happened if he had had to wait out the week?

Let's look at how Jerry handled a similar situation. The main difference between him and Bob is that Jerry is aware of stress and has been through a program in Creative Relaxation.

If worrying is not readily directed into constructive channels, it is a great drain on one's energy supply and causes one to function below a productive level. Before letting worrying build momentum, Jerry proceeded to negate his familiar physical stress reactions by using the Creative Relaxation method.

He began to take control of his thinking by saying things to himself like: "Worrying over something that I am not sure of is a waste of my precious adaptive energy supply." He gathered facts to get a clearer picture of the situation. His top salesman had worked for him ten years. In all of the ten years this salesman had always come to him to talk out problems. The salesman had resisted enticing offers before. Jerry mentally reviewed their last meeting. The meeting was productive, and there were no clear signs that the salesman was displeased. As Jerry continued to focus on the realities of the situation, he was able to worry less and to think more clearly. He stopped fantasizing about the disaster he might face. Next Jerry asked himself the question "What can I do about it?" He figured out several reasonable alternatives. After selecting one, he proceeded to take action. He called his salesman's home again. This time he remembered to ask where they were staying and if they had left a phone number. He had failed to ask for it the first time because surprise and sudden worry immobilized him. Realizing there was a time difference in the place where the salesman was vacationing, Jerry planned on phoning at a time when he thought he might catch his salesman in his hotel room.

Once he had developed a plan of action and had reached

a comfortable stopping point, Jerry rejoined his family in playing their Scrabble tournament and put away thoughts of business. Whenever a thought of uncertainty entered his mind during the game, he would mentally push the play button on his imaginary cassette recorder and the thought would leave. Each time he successfully let the troubling thought go, he would quickly commend himself for his effective channeling of stress. Precious moments of Jerry's life—and his family's—were not eaten up uselessly by the ghost of future stress.

Another stressor the boss often faces involves a stress displacement that I call the Vern Menske syndrome. The Vern Menske syndrome originated with one of my clients whom I'll call Leonard. He was a training manager for a large insurance company. He had a client, Vern Menske, who occasionally would call and complain bitterly about the way Leonard's office was operated. Finally Leonard learned that if he just let Vern talk, he would eventually reveal that something traumatic had happened at his own office. Vern had chosen to complain about Leonard's office because he did not have the authority or courage to complain at his own office. Leonard has learned not to be offended by what Vern says.

The Vern Menske syndrome can be spotted whenever an angry customer or employee transfers his anger or "dumps a bucket" on a third party. Often the third party gets selected as the victim at random or because he has committed a minor error at the wrong time. In many situations the boss becomes the victim of the Vern Menske syndrome. He is commonly the middleman who helps to restore balance in the office when problems arise.

The victims of the Vern Menske syndrome usually develop feelings of frustration, anger, and irritability. They often complain of bad headaches, upset stomachs, or overall feelings of nervousness. Creative Relaxation has been found to help ease these reactions.

It is of prime importance when you experience anger being transferred to you that you maintain your ability to think clearly. In order to use Creative Relaxation here, you first need to keep negating familiar stress reactions. Most people are successful in using Creative Relaxation to help them maintain a smooth pattern of breathing and at the same time to relax specific muscles. Second, keep in mind what it is that you want. It is important that you recognize that the angry person attacking you is operating at an unconscious emotional level. He is attacking you personally for no good reason. Therefore, there's no point in taking his words personally.

The third step is the clincher. You need to communicate effectively with the angry person. It is necessary to listen without interrupting when a person is upset. As you listen, keep clarifying in your mind what is inference and what is fact. When the storm has passed, ask some questions. The questions that you ask should give the person an opportunity either to let out any leftover frustrations or to clarify factual information. Try to avoid phrasing questions in a way that causes the person to become defensive. When you sense that the person is thinking more rationally, ask him what he would like you to do about the problem. This may allow the other to see that you are not the person who can act—he is.

In essence, what you are doing is using Creative Relaxation to help maintain your own optimal stress level as you proceed to lower the stress of the other person. Often we let an upset person raise our stress level, with the result that each ends up attacking the other and the original problem never gets clearly defined. It is at that point that ineffective solutions for the wrong problem emerge.

Let's look at how another manager, Steve, was able to overcome the Vern Menske syndrome. He managed an insurance agency. On the average he had about forty agents working out of his office. On Wednesday morning he came into his office as usual. Everything seemed calm until suddenly Joe, one of his newer agents, stormed angrily into Steve's office, slamming the door behind him. At first Steve was startled by this unexpected explosion. During the six months that Steve had been working with Joe, he had never seen him this upset. Steve began to use his Creative Relaxation skills.

First he sat back in his chair, making sure his body was comfortable. Next, he identified the parts of his body that were becoming tense. Then he checked out his breathing. He negated the undesirable reactions by inhaling deeply and smoothly. As he exhaled he initiated a wave of a calm feeling that started at his head and progressed down to his toes. He continued to breathe smoothly and evenly as he listened attentively to Joe's problem. Joe was upset because he had just found out that another agent in the office who had been with the company only three months had a bookshelf in his office. Joe contended that he had been there twice as long and still did not have bookshelves. Joe felt that it was not fair. Steve wanted to be open, fair, and objective with his people. He also thought Joe was a good insurance agent and recognized that it was important to help keep Joe motivated. Once Steve identified what he wanted, he proceeded to ask Joe some questions.

"From what you've explained, that doesn't seem fair. How did you find out that this other agent has bookshelves in his office?" Steve kept tabs on his stress level throughout the conversation. He called upon that "wave of a calm feeling" and negated any distressful reactions whenever he heard Joe personally attacking him by saying things like

"You really show favoritism. You are like all the rest; you pick favorites and give them everything first."

Steve let Joe get most of his anger out and then calmly said, "Joe, I can see that you are very upset. This isn't like you. Is there anything else that is troubling you?" There was a long period of silence. Finally, Joe confided that last night he had lost his biggest policy sale. He thought his client was going to sign, but sometime between their last appointment and last night the customer decided to go with another company. What made matters worse was that the client let Joe talk for an hour before he told him his decision. By effectively using Creative Relaxation, Steve accomplished what he wanted with his employee and at the same time avoided letting himself be a victim of the Vern Menske syndrome. You can never predict when you will be made a victim of the Vern Menske syndrome by colleagues or family members. Creative Relaxation techniques can save your time—and perhaps your friendships, as well.

THE PROBLEMS OF
A MANAGER

Traditionally businesses were operated by managers giving orders to subordinates. Some new stress arises when employees trained in modern business practices want to take a more active role in decision making. Traditional management today feels threatened by external stressors in the form of younger rivals, higher educational levels, and unfamiliar techniques.

Some other stressors inherent in management roles are the pressure of making deadlines, being caught in the middle of changes in business, the difficulty of delegating responsibilities, and the trials of getting effective follow-through. Limited authority on the one hand and broad responsibility on the other make management a precarious balancing act. Such stressors are not avoidable. The goal is to learn how to cope with them effectively. It is important for a manager to realize that he is not just juggling machines or numbers. When dealing with people, situations are not always clearly defined. The goal of a manager is to figure out what is the most efficient or effective way of dealing with each particular situation.

The following incidents highlight how managers have been able to use Creative Relaxation to help them adjust to external and internal stressors.

A common producer of stress for a manager is the pressure of making deadlines. A telling study conducted by Drs. Friedman and Rosenburg showed that one of the major stressors leading to heart attacks among professionals in three different professional areas was the pressure of making deadlines.

A typical example is a client named Dennis, an auditor. For the past twenty-seven years he has worked for one of the "big three" automotive companies. He is proud that in all his years of service with the company, he has never missed a deadline. But Dennis is getting tired. The feelings of pressure that accompany meeting a deadline were easier to handle when he was young. Now in his fifties, Dennis finds that his body cannot bounce back as it used to. He entered the relaxation program to see if Creative Relaxation could help him let go of the feelings of anxiety and pressure before he left the office.

Whenever Dennis was assigned to a new project, he would carry the frustrations home with him at night. His wife learned to recognize when Dennis was handed a new deadline. The symptoms would grow in proportion to the size of the project. She noticed that Dennis would come home at night more irritable and would take his frustrations out on her. Throughout the evening Dennis would mention that his back was giving him trouble and that his neck felt tight. When they would go to bed at night, his wife would hear him sighing and taking a long time to fall asleep. The reactions were all the result of Dennis's worrying about completing the project by the deadline date.

After learning Creative Relaxation, Dennis learned how to reduce that pressured feeling. First, he realized that he unconsciously associated the success of meeting deadlines with worrying and feeling pressured—that he attributed his success to his worrying. His earlier conditioning had trained him to believe that only successful people worry and that lazy people don't care. Now he accepts that his successes are attributable to the quality of his efforts. He learned that worrying doesn't get a project done; it only unproductively drains one's supply of adaptive energy.

Dennis was able to reap the benefits of Creative Relaxation in the following incident. Dennis came to the office one Wednesday with a full list of tasks to do. As soon as he sat down to work his boss called him into his office. He immediately stopped what he was working on and went to the boss's office. His boss greeted him quickly and went on to present him with a detailed report that he wanted completed by Monday morning. Instead of developing the familiar stress reactions, Dennis inhaled deeply and then he slowly exhaled, relaxing all his muscles from his face to his toes. At the same time he repeated silently to himself, "Relax and stay calm; this must be an important project. You just do it and get it over with, and no complaints." Instead of panicking and wanting to rush out of the office, he stayed there and asked questions about the project. As soon as they finished the discussion, Dennis calmly gathered the materials and went back to his own office. All the while he kept breathing smoothly as he repeated to himself, "Remember to keep positively channeling your adaptive energy supply." Once he got to his desk, he pushed aside the papers that he had planned to work on and replaced them with the materials for the new project. He boasted that he did not waste one second worrying about the project. His feeling of satisfaction mounted inside. He had avoided worrying by paying more attention to his physical and mental signals. Even if he is unaware of negative thoughts, Dennis is now quick to recognize his physical symptoms of stress. He has learned to rechannel his negative thoughts in more positive ways. Dennis now has confidence that he will make it to his retirement year in good shape.

One of the manager's roles is to delegate responsibilities to the people in his department. The manager depends on his staff to carry out various job assignments. His stress level rises quickly when tasks are not completed to his satisfaction.

Whenever you work with other people, stressors are expected to arise. For example, it is five o'clock in the afternoon and you notice that your secretary leaves an important business letter in the typewriter because technically her day ends at five. Or you may find out from an angry customer that one of your installers drilled a three-quarter-inch hole into a customer's kitchen wall in order to run a three-eighths-inch wire into the room. A classic stressor occurs when one of the technicians in a recording studio forgets to push the record button during a live recording session and doesn't notice the error for some time. A manager needs to learn to cope with such situations. Creative Relaxation is obviously a help here.

However, it is important to distinguish between situations that are inherent in a job and stressors that are indirectly created by the manager. A manager who creates stressors where he works is called a "stress carrier." The manager feels pressured and always under the wire, and he passes this tension on to his staff. This kind of negative stress production can be rechanneled in positive ways. Gary has worked as a manager for only three years. Before, he worked as a technician. He was very proficient for his age and was promoted to manager of the department. When he first became interested in Creative Relaxation, he complained that he had too many things to do in the day. He barely even had enough time for a decent lunch.

After his training in Creative Relaxation, it became evident to Gary that he was "picking up the pieces" for his people whenever there was any trouble. His justification was that he felt he could get the job done a lot faster if he did it himself.

Gary's rationalization may have been valid. However, he had a department of thirteen people. When Gary started "picking up the pieces" for thirteen people, plus trying to complete his own job responsibilities, it is no wonder that he felt overloaded. He was overloading himself.

Gary used Creative Relaxation to help him recognize the moments when he began taking other people's responsibilities as his own. Each day before going to lunch, he would practice the Personal Quiet Time for about ten minutes. At the end of the ten-minute session, his mind was clear and he could quickly review the morning's activities. He determined which activities needed to be delegated and which person on his team (other than himself) was the most skilled at handling the task. He repeats the same process at the end of the day.

Gary has found that the department's productivity increased. His staff is more motivated because they are doing tasks that make use of their skills. Gary realized that in the past when he experienced peak stress moments, he would delegate a job to anyone, as long as it got done. The result was that he would get the wrong person for the job. Creative Relaxation gave him the skill to manage the work and people of the office. He did not have to do it all by himself.

An ever-increasing stressor in businesses today is the placement of women in top jobs. Many men feel threatened when women enter their place of work, especially when a company has traditionally been governed and operated by males.

A typical stressful situation arises when a male and a female executive lunch together. Should the woman take an aggressive role, as she does in the office, and order and pay for her own lunch, or should the male take the responsibility? It is interesting to note that in group training sessions professional men and women seldom identify the increase in stress level that occurs when lunching together. However, after the thought is introduced, both sexes admit that it is a stress point. Men have traditionally done the ordering in restaurants and are used to seeing that a woman's needs are met. A woman's independent behavior may be interpreted by a man as aggressive when she is at the same professional level in the organizational structure and they are competing for similar goals.

The stress that is unknowingly created is negative. The women involved are often described as too aggressive and as taking "this women's lib thing" too far. The stress is usually stored, but it reveals itself back in the office. The female executive often finds that male colleagues are more resistant and less cooperative.

An executive named Gloria found that she more easily gained the respect of her male colleagues by using Creative Relaxation when she ate lunch with them. She would first lower her own stress level by practicing the step of exhaling smoothly and at the same time relaxing the muscles in her body. Reducing her stress level increased Gloria's awareness of how other people were responding to her. She was also more sensitive to signs of stress in others. Once she recognized these responses, she proceeded to take steps to help lower their stress to a more comfortable level.

Gloria recalled a situation in which Ned, another executive in the company, invited her to lunch to discuss the involvement of her department in the new expansion project and how merging departments on this new company project might ease the sales pressure. During the lunch Gloria recognized that Ned preferred being in control. The first signal came when he asked her what she was planning to order from the menu. The second signal was when the waitress asked what she wanted for lunch. The waitress directed her attention to Gloria, and without hesitating Gloria recited exactly what she had just finished telling Ned that she wanted for lunch. She noticed that when she started to place the order with the waitress, Ned started to speak. He quickly covered it up by acting as if he needed to clear his throat, as he adjusted his tie. The third signal was that as soon as the waitress received the order and walked away from the table, Ned continued to discuss the business at hand. Only now his tone of voice was sharper and he enunciated each word more distinctly.

At that point Gloria decided to verify whether her assumptions were correct. She told Ned that she felt a little awkward and wondered if her ordering her own lunch had offended him. He looked at her with surprise, but immediately smiled. At the same time Gloria noticed his chest relax. He complimented her for her perceptiveness and sensitivity to other people. He said that he didn't really mind, but that he was used to ordering for a woman in social situations, and it was a new experience for him to have a woman as a colleague.

Gloria had learned the art of balancing as a result of using Creative Relaxation. She became more flexible and was able to assess when it was important for her to emphasize her professional abilities to others and when it was more productive for her to concentrate on helping to ease the stress of her colleagues. The result was that over the next two years, Gloria moved up the company ladder quickly and with each promotion met little resistance. She was never criticized for being too forceful or trying to throw her weight around. Other women in the work force who are increasing their sensitivity to stress levels in their male colleagues are finding similar results.

An external stressor that frequently creates stress for a manager is the international economic market. Take Ken, the manager of the purchasing department of a large corporation. When Ken came into the office on Monday morning, he was told that the dollar value overseas had taken another drop. As soon as he heard the news, the familiar stress reactions were produced. His face wrinkled and looked solemn, his stomach felt nauseated, and the muscles in his neck and shoulders tightened. The feelings lingered throughout the day.

The drawn look on Ken's face was not unique to that particular Monday. He noticed that each day it became harder to motivate himself. He kept waiting for conditions to stabilize. They never did. As he began to realize this, the feelings of hopelessness kept creeping in.

The training in Creative Relaxation helped Ken to accept that the changing dollar value on the international market was out of his control. He realized that he was no longer living for today. He kept looking for the ideal time, and unknowingly he kept holding himself back in anticipation of when that time would arise. He decided to focus on today. Ken realized that he had control of the day-to-day operations in his department and that was where he needed to direct his energies. Whenever he felt the familiar feelings of hopelessness returning, he would calmly stop what he was doing and negate the negative stress reactions by using the Creative Relaxation techniques that he had learned. Sometimes he found it helpful to tell himself that worrying about something that was out of his control was a waste of his adaptive energy. He further reasoned that the important thing was to do something and make the best of it. And he did.

EMPLOYEE STRESSORS

The lowest man in the organizational structure is the employee. The employee has no control over the definition of job responsibilities. He does not function in a leadership or in a decision-making capacity. Instead, he is responsible for carrying out the orders dictated to him by people higher up in the organization. Even though the employee has little authority in the decision-making process, he is not exempt from stressors on the job.

The external forces of today, like inflation, depletion of our natural resources, and job unemployment, have a marked effect on the employee. However, the internal stressors that arise each day have a more dramatic, tangible effect on an employee. Internal stressors that an employee most frequently faces are troubles with the boss, dissatisfaction with job responsibilities, and the frustration that results from having to contend with a rapidly changing economic system. The employee reacts to today's stressors by complaining about being bored and feeling little or no commitment to the job. As a result, employees tend to be more careless on the job, frequently call in sick, and come to work late.

A common source of frustration for the employee is the boss. There are many types of bosses who create stress for employees. The following examples illustrate three of the most common types.

A typical stress-producing boss is the perfectionist. This boss is often described by employees as being very critical and negative. A perfectionistic boss goes about his work very methodically and systematically. He prefers to complete one project at a time, which includes finishing every minute detail, before going on to the next task. A typical example is opening the mail. A perfectionist would like to be able to sit down and open *all* the mail at one time and respond to *all* the appropriate letters before moving on to the next project. The frustration for the employee is increased when the perfectionistic boss expects the same high level of performance from his subordinates. Employees in this type of working environment often feel pressured. They complain that their boss seldom compliments them on their work. Instead, the boss is quick to find fault in the work that they do. The employee begins to question his own abilities. He interprets the contributions he makes to the company as meaningless. Frequently, the employee will torment himself by wondering, "Is it all worth it?"

Hunter is an example of an employee who works for a perfectionist. For three years Hunter has worked as an assistant to the manager of an office supply firm. He complained that in addition to the characteristics mentioned above, this boss would yell at him about how he handled a particular situation and then go off and do the very same thing. Nevertheless, Hunter learned how to use Creative Relaxation to cope with this type of boss.

If this is your situation at work, then you should follow each of the steps in the Pendulum Concept of stress, as Hunter did. He found that the best time to go through the steps was immediately after finishing the Personal Quiet Time, when his mind was clearer and more alert. First Hunter decided that he wanted to continue to work for this company. In order to be a candidate for further career advancements, he needed the experience. His second conclusion was that financially he could not afford to quit. He recently had bought some new furniture and he needed a guaranteed source of income to pay the bills that kept coming in monthly. Since Hunter could not walk away from the stressor, he had to minimize the damage it could do to him.

Hunter could see that his boss was his major source of stress. As a result of his training in Creative Relaxation, Hunter realized that he needed to be more specific. He narrowed the source of his stress to two specific stressors. One was that his boss always looked at his work in a critical way. The other was that his boss never seemed to compliment him.

Hunter began to associate the presence of his physical symptoms with these stressors. He realized that after meeting with his boss, he would walk back to his desk with an upset stomach. Invariably by the end of the day he would be suffering from a pounding headache. When he got home at night he was irritable with his wife and children and would snap back at them for the slightest thing.

Realizing that he wasn't going to change his job or his boss, Hunter learned to deal with the situation by making the following adjustments. First, whenever his boss criticized him, Hunter would not let it affect him personally. He realized that his boss criticized others to fulfill his need always to be perfect. Hunter replaced the negative comments from his boss with positive thoughts about himself. At the same time, he negated his physical stress reactions by inhaling and then relaxing his muscles as he smoothly exhaled. He also helped to maintain a balanced stress level by periodically repeating silently to himself, "Think positive and you are positive."

Hunter noticed a marked difference in his attitude toward his boss. For instance, Hunter had been devoting a lot of time to writing out a three-month project proposal for the firm. His boss asked to see how the proposal was going. He proudly handed him the proposal, momentarily forgetting the critical nature of his boss. Moments after receiving the proposal, the boss criticized Hunter for not having the pages numbered and for not including a table of contents. The quality of the content of the proposal was never mentioned. At first, as the boss criticized him, thoughts of disgust raced through Hunter's mind. He began to check his muscles for signs of physical stress as he thought about his boss's unending desire for perfection. Pity for the boss's need to criticize took hold in Hunter's mind. He noticed that physically his heart was pounding and that his breathing was short and choppy. Instantly he negated the physical reactions by producing a "wave of a calm feeling" throughout his body as he exhaled.

Hunter noticed that he was able to stay more objective and keep the conversation focused on the business at hand. Instead of defending himself, which always led him into a quarrel, he simply agreed with his boss that the proposal did need a table of contents and that the pages should be numbered. To Hunter's amazement, his boss quickly dropped the conversation. Afterward Hunter reviewed the situation to try to figure out why his boss had responded in this way. Hunter concluded that whenever he attempted to defend himself and quarrel with the boss, he was overconcerned that his boss wasn't listening to his opinions. But at that moment his boss really didn't care about Hunter's point of view. He was only interested in pointing out to Hunter the weaknesses in the proposal. Hunter changed his attitude and eliminated the physical symptoms. To his surprise, he got along better with his boss.

Another type of boss who adds to employee stress is the boss who takes an idea from an employee and claims it as his own. A person who has this tendency frequently puts his staff in an uncomfortable position. Should the employee confront the boss and let him know whose idea it really is, or should he let it pass? The employee's stress increases when he chooses not to make a decision and at the same time carries a grudge for several days.

Theodora typifies this kind of employee. She is in her late forties and for the past ten years has worked as a nurse. Her current supervisor has the habit of incorporating Theodora's ideas as her own. Whenever an idea of Theodora's is presented by her supervisor at one of their meetings, Theodora sits there and stews. Theodora said that she has the tremendous urge at that moment to jump out of her seat and wave her arms, exclaiming that she is the rightful owner of that idea. Instead, she suppresses the urge. The bottled-up stress is carried for several days afterward. She is irritable with others at work throughout the day. At night, she has difficulty falling asleep because her anger seems to surface at that time. For several days she feels tightness in her neck.

If you are in a similar work environment, the first thing you need to do is to define your short-term and long-term goals. Next you need to assess how important it is to you to point out to your boss that the ideas are your own. More important, you need to learn how to let go of that lingering grudge. Many people have succeeded in letting go of a grudge by looking at the situation from a positive angle. For instance, if you are one of a select few from whom the boss regularly borrows ideas, then your ideas must be pretty good ones. If your boss decides to implement your ideas, are you not better off?

It is important that you choose a particular course of action. A lot of adaptive energy can be wasted by sulking each time the situation arises. Establish a plan of action. This lowers stress by reducing the uncertainty of how you react.

It is interesting to note the many different opinions on how to handle this kind of boss. In a recent survey, approximately 50 percent of the respondents thought that it was important to let the boss know that the ideas were theirs. Everyone agreed that it should be done in private and quickly, while the idea was still fresh in everyone's mind. A large percentage felt that even if it meant sacrificing their job, they would let their boss know.

On the other hand, a large group felt that they would not tell their boss. These people questioned what they would gain by pointing out the real source of the idea. Some feared rocking the boat. If the boss was likely to give them a hard time, then the price was too high. Others reasoned that as long as you are getting what you want, it makes no difference who gets credit for the ideas.

Theodora decided to handle the situation in the following way. First, Theodora eliminated her three-day grudge. She admitted to herself that she was angry. However, holding a grudge for three days didn't eliminate the stressor. Next she decided to write out her ideas and send them to her supervisor as a memo. She kept a copy for her records. Theodora decided that she would point out to her boss only the important ideas. The other, less significant ideas she would not bring up.

The next time her supervisor mentioned one of Theodora's ideas at a meeting, Theodora sat calmly back in her chair. After the meeting she strategically arranged a casual conversation with her supervisor. Theodora complimented her supervisor on the good meeting and how pleased she was that her supervisor thought enough of her idea that she decided to share it with the other nurses. The supervisor was not insulted and Theodora got the satisfaction of claiming credit for her own ideas.

Whenever an employee is faced with a new boss, certain changes and adjustments are necessary. A certain amount of stress is created just by the presence of a new boss. However, when the new boss introduces changes in the structure too quickly or when the traditional ways of doing things are no longer acceptable, employees initially react by feeling threatened. Many employees are fearful because they are afraid of the unknown. They question whether they will be able to work comfortably and adequately under the new conditions. The pressure mounts as the employee realizes the squeeze play between the need to keep a job and the need to escape stress.

The outcome is a decrease in motivation, efficiency, and productivity. Employees are more irritable and less cooperative. There is an increase in physical complaints. Frequently, the feelings of discomfort are transferred into their private lives. Their loved ones become the innocent victims of their distress.

Morris, for example, had worked for the same real estate firm for more than twelve years. He had always worked for the same boss, and he liked the way things in the office were done. One day his boss surprised him by announcing that he was leaving. The person who took his place was a middle-aged boss who had visions of shaping things up. Morris noticed after working with this new boss that he would come home at night more irritable. Other notable changes were that Morris had frequent headaches and always felt tired.

Morris turned to Creative Relaxation because of his headaches. He preferred using a relaxation technique to control his headaches to taking drugs.

During one of our sessions, Morris started discussing the stressors at work. He was quite confident that the major source of his stress was his new boss. However, when I inquired further, Morris realized that the major stressor was not his boss, but change. In the final analysis, Morris was able to relate fairly well to his new boss as a person. The difficulty was in adjusting to the numerous changes that were taking place on the job.

Once Morris recognized the actual source of his stress, he felt immediate relief. The next time he felt the familiar stress reactions, he asked himself if the stressor was the idea of change or the actual situation to be handled.

For example, Morris's new boss implemented a company policy that all employees had to wear matching blazers. Each employee was to wear a name tag above the upper left pocket. Morris felt the beginning symptoms of a headache. Immediately, he knew that something was wrong. That afternoon, at the end of his Personal Quiet Time, he asked himself why he felt so uptight. He could not come up with a substantial reason to justify the negative feelings. He then realized that he was resisting change. He found that he could benefit by using the familiar physical reactions as a signal to check out what was going on around him and to help him identify the stressor.

As a result, Morris was able to adjust more easily to new

situations. He discovered that after earnestly trying to follow a new procedure, he could discuss any objections that he might have from a more practical, objective point of view.

The next time you find yourself confronted with change, you might try considering the following points:

1. Become aware of how you react. Are you being resistant? If so, identify your source of resistance. Is it change, or is it that you are uncomfortable with what is being asked of you?
2. Assess your sources of information. Are you resisting a new policy because you heard other people criticizing it? Are your judgments based on established fact or on what you think to be true?
3. Become aware of your attitude. Are you standing on the sidelines waiting for the change to prove itself before you become a believer? Are you approaching the change objectively and channeling your energies in a positive direction before evaluating the outcome?

Morris and many other people have found that practicing the Personal Quiet Time assists them in recognizing their specific stress reactions. They can more easily identify the sources of their stress. Many people have been able to determine whether they are adding to the stress. By integrating the technique into their day, people are able to adjust more easily to change.

With the growing numbers of young people entering the job market and with many others switching careers, stress is created when employees are repeatedly told, "But you lack experience." For many employees, this is a stressful situation because they feel that their ideas are being rejected and their lack of experience on the job is just an excuse.

Employees who feel this way quickly lose their glow of enthusiasm and creativity. Eventually, for survival purposes, they mold themselves to resemble the vast majority of employees who view their work as "just a job."

Women frequently face the criticism that they lack necessary job experience. One example is Joan, a bright woman in her late twenties. When she first tried Creative Relaxation, she had just started working for a real estate company. She was the only woman in an office full of experienced real estate salesmen. The men did not value any comments or suggestions that Joan made. They all decided beforehand that, because of her inexperience, her ideas were not backed by the necessary expertise.

Joan acknowledged the fact that she lacked experience. She was also willing to put up with sly comments about "the new addition" to the office. Her goal of learning the real estate trade outweighed the small psychological points the men made at her expense. In a relatively short period of time, her experience caught up with her intelligence and she proved herself as competent as her colleagues.

Even though Joan understood the dynamics of what was happening, it still bothered her. She benefited by using Creative Relaxation to help her unwind at the end of the day. She was able to keep her goals in focus more easily. This helped her to avoid taking personally the comments made about her by her colleagues.

Joan worked for the company only a short while before quitting her job. She did not leave because of the ridicule directed against her. She left because she had reached her goal and was finding that she was getting bored. She started her own company and within two years she hired one of her old "critics" as an agent.

THE STRESSORS OF A
SALESPERSON

Salespeople often have to face the same stressors of other business people plus some stressors unique to their profession. There are many stressors in selling. The following four examples illustrate a few of the more frequent ones.

- A salesperson can work several days to try to meet a client and discover when they do meet that the client has just bought the product from another company.
- An even more frustrating situation arises when you have already been working with a customer and instead of signing the final contract agreement with you, he announces that he has decided to go with another company.
- Other frustrations appear when weeks pass and you haven't made that big sale.
- A classic stress-producing event that most new salespeople describe follows a pattern. They go through an entire forty-five-minute presentation to a client, only to find out that they were talking to the wrong person.

One of the most common problems for a salesperson is unwinding at the end of a day. Each morning as the eager salesperson leaves for work he begins psyching himself up for the day ahead. Many salespeople have developed the fine art of motivating themselves, yet few have the ability easily and effectively to "turn their motors off" at will.

One successful salesperson, David, used to unwind at the end of the day by stopping off on the way home and having a "tall blond one"—a tall, cold glass of beer. Nevertheless, it took David about two to three hours to unwind each night. There were many evenings when he would be sound asleep by the time the evening news came on the television set. David found that living at this pace was beginning to take its toll. He was earning a healthy income and provided his family with all the niceties of life. However, he was beginning to ask himself what value all this money had, if he risked not living long enough to spend it, much less enjoy it.

David's prime interest in learning Creative Relaxation was to help him unwind at the end of a day. After the first session in Creative Relaxation, he found immediate relief. The muscles in his body felt limp and heavy. At the same time he noticed that his thoughts had slowed down.

At our next meeting, David complained that even though he benefited after each experience in the Personal Quiet Time, he could not find the time to practice it. He explained that each day was unpredictable and that no two days were alike. It was difficult for him to find even one twenty-minute period in his day to practice the PQT. At that point in his training, David realized that the challenge was not to learn Creative Relaxation, but to practice the technique daily. It was pointed out to David that he can't just find the time if his life is really hectic. He needs to make the time. At present, his day is already filled with tasks and responsibilities. He does not have a twenty-minute time slot open each day. Therefore, he needs to plan, to schedule a slot to practice the technique. He needs to learn to do it as regularly as he brushes his teeth. By the end of his training, David developed the Creative Relaxation habit at the end of his working day, whenever his day ended.

Most of the time, David was on the road and worked out of his car. Before starting his drive home he would sit in his parked car and go through the Personal Quiet Time. He would play music from a cassette on his car tape deck. For twenty minutes he would comfortably sit back and go through one of the Progressions. On the days when he felt inspired, he would drive to a picturesque place and do the technique.

He found that as he became more proficient in the technique, he could more easily unwind. He noticed that he drove home at night feeling more refreshed and alert. On many occasions he would create new ways to improve his sales presentation. An added bonus was that David lost fifteen unwanted pounds that he had gained, because he didn't need the tall blond ones anymore.

A major stressor of salespeople is indecision. The stress level rises as the number of "maybes" accumulates. As the end of the month approaches and as the bills start coming in, the stress level reaches its peak. Any salesperson knows that he can't take a "maybe" to the bank.

Each time a customer gives a maybe, a salesperson must follow up and get back to the customer. When a salesperson gets a long list of maybes, the majority of his time is spent in retracing old steps. It becomes progressively more difficult to have the time to find the new customer who is ready to buy.

The salesperson in this situation is frequently the source of his own stress. The stress that is produced is the result of his attempt to avoid hearing a customer say no. When a salesperson is face to face with a client, he would rather wait and get no decision than have the customer say no. In the selling profession this is called fear of rejection. When a salesperson suffers from fear of rejection, he will unconsciously fail to close a deal or will put off asking the customer for payment.

Exchanging a "no" for a "maybe" is a temporary reliever of stress. However, the maybes produce greater stress in the long run. The reason is that unpredictability is increased. It has been found that as unpredictability increases, so does stress. Therefore, the more maybes that a salesperson creates, the more the unpredictability increases, and the more unpredictability, the greater the stress.

The net result is a decrease in energy, sales, and motivation. This alone is powerful enough to discourage a new salesperson from continuing.

Rosa, a newcomer to a sales department, was able to minimize the feelings that accompanied a rejection by using Creative Relaxation in the following ways. First, when she received a rejection, she would give herself a certain amount of time to feel bad. As she drove in her car to her next appointment, Rosa would allow herself five minutes of remorse. During the five-minute period, she would review in her mind how she could have improved her presentation. At the end of the five minutes, she would simply forget the situation by discarding it, retaining only those points that were of value. If the incident tried to reenter her mind, she simply would let go of the thought by using the techniques learned from the Personal Quiet Time.

Instead of following her natural instincts of running away after hearing her customer say no, Rosa was able to maintain her optimal stress level by incorporating Creative Relaxation and to stay long enough with the client to ask him for any referrals. Practicing this approach helped her get additional sales.

After receiving a rejection, Rosa also found it helpful to use Creative Relaxation to help her replace negative thoughts with more positive ones. She had two positive thoughts that were effective in helping her avoid depression. First, she recalled that the selling profession is a numbers game. Realistically, she can't sell to every customer. Also, she realized that it was far better to have a customer convinced on his own accord, rather than her doing the convincing for him. Rosa realized that she sells a particular product only once; but she gains a customer for life. She would review these thoughts in her mind at the same time that she relaxed the muscles throughout her body.

Another stressor for a salesperson is cold calls. A cold call is when a salesperson calls a potential client for the first time. Its purpose is either to commit the client to buying your product or service at the time of the call or to have the client agree to meet with you to discuss business at a later date.

A salesperson who does not make cold calls is said to suffer from "call reluctance." The first symptom of call reluctance is present when the salesperson just cannot get around to making his calls. The general pattern is that with every attempt to phone a potential customer, something always gets in the salesperson's way. The pattern usually begins in the morning. The thought to call clients in the morning is postponed because the salesperson concludes that it is too early in the morning to make calls and that it would be better to wait. The next thought of making calls comes around one o'clock in the afternoon. But the salesperson figures that he would be wasting his time because most of the people he needs to talk to are probably not back from lunch.

Conveniently, the thought reenters his mind around 4:30. At that time the salesperson convinces himself that he is now ready. By the time he gets all the names and phone numbers in front of him it's 4:50. He ends his phone calling at 5:00 P.M. sharp, telling himself that the people he needs to speak to leave the office at that time. This game is played day after day. It is costly to both the salesperson and the company. This stressor of making cold calls is a necessary component of successful selling. To channel stress successfully in this situation does not mean to avoid the stressor, but instead to learn how to deal effectively with it.

A young man named Ron exemplifies an eager, energetic salesperson who dislikes making cold calls. When he personally meets with a client, he feels quite confident and is able to talk freely. However, Ron acts very differently when he is on the phone. He feels uncomfortable and insecure because he is not able to see how the client is reacting. Whenever he called a client for the first time, he actually prayed that his client would not be available. A feeling of panic overwhelmed him when the secretary transferred his call to the client. Each second that Ron had to wait was magnified into a minute. His heart would start to throb, his breathing became irregular, as he felt the muscles tightening in his chest and throat. When the moment arrived for Ron to speak, his voice would either quiver or crack.

Ron tried Creative Relaxation as a result of his boss's recommendation. He learned to eliminate the fear that accompanied making a cold call by implementing three steps that he created as a result of his training in Creative Relaxation. Before placing a call, he would review the worst possible thing that could happen—a no. Immediately, he rationalized that no was only a word. He learned during the training sessions to imagine the word no, and the feelings of rejection that accompanied the word, as a piece of lint. Whenever a customer told him no, Ron would swiftly imagine that piece of lint on his suit. He was able to eliminate any hurt feelings or feelings of rejection by simply brushing the lint off his suit.

Second, as he dialed the phone he maintained a smooth pattern of breathing and periodically he would create a "wave of a calm feeling" throughout his body. The third step that helped Ron to feel more confident was to imagine as the phone was ringing that he was sitting and casually talking to another person in the same room. He was able to do this easily as the phone was ringing because he had learned from the Personal Quiet Time settings how to visualize imaginative scenes.

Ron found that his voice no longer cracked or quivered. As his confidence increased, he made more cold calls. Ron now has more opportunities to present his product. His number of weekly sales has increased dramatically.

He told me that he still doesn't *like* to make cold calls. It is not as natural to him as talking to someone in person. The difference is that now he can be effective and confident in spite of his dislike for making cold calls.

STRESSORS OF A SECRETARY

One of the most important persons in a corporation, business, or organization is the secretary. Most of the secretary's stresses come from three sources: the customer, the boss, and job definition. The first stressor is the customer. Many businesses fail to recognize that the secretary is often the first person that a customer meets and is thus the one who forms a customer's first impression of the company. The secretary is also on the company's front line for any irate customers. Frequently, a secretary has the responsibility of calming down an angry client. Many times she is forced into the situation because of her position at the front desk or on the phone. In addition, the responsibilities of trying to meet report deadlines, getting everything done in a day, and trying to handle many things all at once are inherent in a secretary's job and create stress.

On a routine basis the most frequent source of stress for the secretary is the people she works for. From her perspective, many things that her boss does create stress. The following examples typify some of the more common kinds of stressful situations that a secretary faces.

A secretary may come to her desk in the morning and see a stack of work to be typed. She is told that all the reports are "top priority." The situation often becomes overwhelming when she works for more than one boss and they all turn in their very important reports at the same time to be typed. Understandably, the secretary's job becomes very frustrating.

Sara is an example of one secretary who had the problem of work pile-ups. She works for several members of the professional staff in a large accounting firm. Frequently, she would come into the office and find a stack of papers on her desk. She would start typing the reports in the order she received them. Her frustration level would reach its peak when one of her bosses would complain to her that she had typed the wrong report first.

By the time Sara decided to receive training in Creative Relaxation, she was feeling uptight all the time. She dreaded going to work. By the time Sara had finished Progression III, she was already learning ways to channel stress more positively at work.

She found that practicing the Personal Quiet Time helped her slow down enough to think. Learning how to stop herself from becoming upset enabled her to see the problem clearly. She realized that she needed to figure out a way to set priorities in her work. This would help to eliminate much of her stress and would satisfy her bosses. She decided that since her bosses were not telling her which reports were most important, she was going to ask, every time. Each time Sara was handed a report from one of her bosses, she would politely ask him the day, and time, if necessary, that he needed the typing completed. If there appeared to be a conflict in meeting the deadlines, she would further question a particular boss about the importance of the report and its deadline date.

For the reports that were turned in when she was away from her desk, she developed a simple form that her bosses filled out. They merely indicated their "preferred" date and "must" date of completion and initialed the form. The outcome was that her bosses were happier because they were getting their reports on time. Sara was pleased because she suffered less irritation on the job. Another difference that she noted by regularly practicing the Personal Quiet Time was that her typing speed and accuracy improved, since her mind was not cluttered with distractions while she typed.

A second stressor arises when, for example, a boss walks past the copying machine to come into his secretary's office to hand her one sheet of paper for her to make one copy. Such thoughtless bosses can wear out even the best secretary. One secretary who worked in this kind of setting said she would come "unglued" when she had to stop typing dictation to copy one sheet of paper. She contended that this was an inefficient way to use a secretary's skills.

Similar stresses are created when a secretary is asked to perform extra personal services for her boss. For instance, she may be asked to help him by purchasing a few gifts from the boss's long Christmas list or getting a birthday card for his wife or stopping off at his bank to make a quick deposit for him. Other extra duties may include dusting off the boss's desk in the morning or emptying his ashtrays. Some secretaries resent having to make coffee for their boss each morning. Secretaries who work in this type of setting often complain about feeling degraded. They feel subservient to their boss. Many feel frustrated because they are not able to use their skills to their full capacity.

Creative Relaxation training helped Carmen to cope with these negative feelings. She enjoyed being a secretary and, for the most part, she enjoyed working for her boss. She concluded that as long as she decided to stay with her boss, she needed to change the way she reacted and to stop thinking of herself as subservient. She learned from Creative Relaxation to differentiate stress levels. She would use that as a gauge to help her determine when she needed to take action and mention her distress. Before Creative Relaxation, she allowed the feelings of resentment to accumulate. When she got home at night she would complain to her husband or withdraw in a depressed mood.

Now when Carmen finds herself putting in extra time to do her regular activities because she has been helping her boss with some personal favors, she feels more comfortable and justified in asking him for some time off. Before, she would bury that resentment inside as she waited for her boss to offer her some time off. If her job responsibilities become too great, she no longer struggles to try to meet the demands of the job. Instead, she goes to her boss and suggests several options that would make her job easier. Carmen found that by trying this new approach, she felt more positive about herself and about her job.

There are times when a secretary feels grumpy and is difficult to get along with, and doesn't know why. One secretary, Marilyn, explained that by ten o'clock in the morning she felt irritable, headachy, and angry. For the next two hours she was difficult to work with. The pressured feeling made it difficult for her to figure out the source of her stress. She turned to Creative Relaxation to help her unwind so that she could stop the momentum of the morning and determine the source of her stress. She found that by negating the physical reactions to stress, she was able to identify three potential sources of stress: her boss, the job duties, and her own attitude.

In order to assess fairly the overall situation at work,

Marilyn needed to determine if she was receiving enough satisfaction on the job to make up for the irritation. Once having made this assessment, she would need to face either quitting her job or taking active steps to make some changes at her place of work. It was suggested to her during Creative Relaxation training that she needed to develop a course of action. The plan she came up with took Marilyn one week to complete. For one day only, after she completed the Personal Quiet Time, she compiled a list of her frustrations on the job. On the second day, after she finished practicing the Personal Quiet Time, she compiled a list of job satisfactions. For the next two days she was advised to not think about any of the items on the lists. At the end of the two days, she sat down after the Personal Quiet Time, compared the two lists, and developed a third list of alternatives. How could she increase the satisfactions list and shorten the frustrations list?

The next step after determining her alternatives was to take action. Marilyn was so certain that her job frustrations were unbearable that she decided to quit. She promptly brought these items to her boss's attention, with the thought of leaving her job. Marilyn was pleasantly surprised to discover that a new alternative emerged. Her boss pointed out that he had not been aware of how she felt and was quite willing to make adjustments in her job and speak to the other employees who added to her work load.

Since she decided to stay on the job, the next course of action was to determine more specifically the stressors that she needed to change. Marilyn chose not to tackle immediately the most difficult stressor. Instead, she practiced a short ten-minute Personal Quiet Time session. Afterward she sat back and organized her thoughts about typing reports. She figured out that her major source of stress in typing reports was not having all the information included in the original draft. She decided that before typing a report she needed to determine what information was needed. Next, she called the appropriate person and established a convenient time when she could expect to have the information. While she was waiting for the information she proceeded to type the sections of the report that were completed. She found that the typing went more smoothly and that she had fewer interruptions bothering her.

After several weeks had passed, Marilyn commented on how pleased she was to have learned some specific skills that she could effectively use to help her face some of life's real stressors. Her boss was pleased because he knew that she was taking an active role in increasing her own job satisfaction.

Some of the conclusions that you may reach after following the guidelines presented in this chapter may seem drastic: standing up to your boss, realizing that you may be a stress carrier, planning to quit your job. If you are able to overcome your fears and grapple with problems on the job, then you have come a long way on the road to a positive and satisfying life. But if there is any area of life in which stress and fear cause more problems than in the office, it is in the bedroom. The skills that you have learned so far will be needed to help you to confront these problems in the next chapter.

9 ❀ Better Sex through Creative Relaxation

The "balanced" men and women who have learned to practice Creative Relaxation effectively in contacts with their friends, co-workers, and family members may sometimes find that they are still experiencing some difficulties in their most intimate relationships. This situation is not uncommon, and it is perfectly understandable. For the most part, sexual response and sexual pleasure are natural and instinctual. But our physical behavior is also strongly influenced by our thoughts and emotions. Everyone isn't automatically a good lover. Sexual technique is partially a learned ability. At the most basic level we have to learn how to get the most out of our lovemaking. Because our relationships with our wives or husbands or lovers are close and important to us, we sometimes find it hard to achieve and maintain emotional and physical equilibrium when our relationship is subjected to stress. Any number of factors may interfere with sexual functioning, affecting our ability to create a mutually pleasurable relationship with our sexual partner.

The idea of using Creative Relaxation to improve or enhance sexual functioning first came from one of my patients. I met her in the hall late one afternoon after I had finished a meeting and was walking back to my office in the hospital. She had recently been discharged and wanted to pick up some artwork she had left behind. As I was about to open the door to the art room, she placed her hand on my arm and said shyly: "I want to thank you for the help you gave me through Creative Relaxation, and so does my husband. I am able to use the technique to help me relax when we make love. For the first time in years I have no painful discomfort." That was the beginning.

Creative Relaxation is not a magical cure for severe sexual disabilities any more than it is a solution for any other major emotional or physical conflict. There are, however, some sexual difficulties that are commonly experienced by people who are physically healthy and seem well adjusted in other respects. My experience has shown that these problems can be alleviated or even eradicated by using Creative Relaxation. And, of course, even a person who already has a satisfactory sex life will appreciate improving it. As someone once said to me, "Creative Relaxation is to sex what a scoop of ice cream is to a slice of warm apple pie. Each is good by itself, but together they are divine."

The most obvious sexual difficulties are those that reveal themselves in some kind of physical symptom. Persons who have no organic disease or handicap can still suffer from *sexual dysfunction*, or problems in sexual response. In men, such dysfunctions include impotence, premature ejaculation, and retarded ejaculation. Impotence, simply defined, results from an insufficient congestion of blood in the penile blood vessels. The impotent man may be able to ejaculate, but his penis fails to elongate and become hard. In cases of premature and retarded ejaculation, a man has a normal erection, but suffers from inadequate control over his physical responses. Premature ejaculation occurs when he does not have sufficient voluntary control over his reflexes, and the result is a too rapid climax. In contrast, retarded ejaculation results from involuntary overcontrol. Even though he receives adequate stimulation, he has trouble releasing his ejaculatory reflex.

Women may also experience forms of sexual dysfunction. One of these, called vaginismus, has no analogy in the male. The condition occurs when the muscles of the vaginal entrance involuntarily contract in response to any attempt at penetration. Obviously, intercourse thus becomes painful and virtually impossible. Two other female sexual dysfunctions are similar to the male problems of impotence and retarded ejaculation. Like the impotent man, the generally unresponsive female (the so-called frigid woman) fails to react adequately to sexual stimulation. She does not show the signs of physiological arousal. For instance, her vagina remains relatively dry and does not lubricate even though her partner has stimulated her and they have intercourse. An unresponsive woman feels no erotic sensation or sexual pleasure at all. And like the male who experiences retarded ejaculation, a woman may have difficulty releasing her orgasmic reflex, even though she is otherwise sexually responsive.

Basically, most of the causes of sexual difficulty lie on a continuum ranging from the superficial fear of failure to extreme sexual dysfunction. Most people experience some difficulty, but only rarely. They are, however, aware that their sex lives are not always completely satisfactory. Too frequently they are not responding as pleasurably as they might. Most sexual problems, in fact, result from a combination of cultural and personal causes. For example, although it is often said that Americans are more sexually free than ever before, modern society still fosters ignorance, myths, and misconceptions about male and female sexual functioning. Old ideas about the "proper" and "natural" masculine and feminine roles die slowly. Many individuals still believe that the only normal pattern for sexual relations is that which follows a set formula consisting of foreplay, intercourse, and male orgasm. The female response may not even be considered.

Even people who consider themselves "liberated" may have only substituted new myths for the old ones and believe that each sexual encounter should produce new heights of ecstasy. In this case, as Helen Singer Kaplan points out in *The Illustrated Manual of Sex Therapy*, the discrepancy between what they really experience and their unrealistic expectations generates much anxiety and guilt. These stressful emotions can ruin an otherwise good relationship. Guilt and anxiety may also cause a person to restrict his sexual activity or even avoid sex altogether.

Guilt and anxiety are not the only culprits. All kinds of negative emotions and unresolved business or personal worries easily disrupt or prevent sexual response. Low self-esteem in one of the sexual partners is a common source of difficulty. A partner who habitually imports outside worries into erotic situations can be devastating to the sexual relationship.

Often these two factors—low self-esteem and an inability to set daily concerns aside for a while—are closely connected. That may be the situation of the business executive who has had a bad day at work. He leaves his office worried about a lost contract and thinking that he has failed himself and the company. The conflicts and bad feelings that he has about himself are likely to carry over into his lovemaking. He has a negative impression of himself and he may continue to brood about the day's events and what he will have to face the next day. The sexual outcome is that he can't perform. He then says to himself, "I knew it. I can't do anything right." His image of himself as inadequate is reinforced, and he may be on the path to recurrent impotence.

Creative Relaxation is applicable across a broad spectrum, from solving sexual problems to further developing the pleasures of the sexual experience. You can use the components of the technique while making love to help you become more physically and emotionally relaxed and to help you to let go of thoughts that might inhibit you. In this way you can learn to dissociate yourself from daily problems so that you don't carry them over into sex. By using the technique to relax, you can achieve more physical comfort and pleasure and can give yourself up to the erotic experience. The case studies that follow illustrate how other people have been able to improve their sexual relationships by practicing Creative Relaxation.

"I've Lost My Sense of Touch"

Darlene was a young woman in her late twenties, married for four years, who said she loved her husband, Jim, dearly. She was delighted to show her affection in sensual ways, bathing before he came home from work, dressing suggestively, and serving lavish meals accompanied by candlelight and soft music. Yet after the first few months of marriage, Darlene could never really let herself unwind enough to enjoy the sexual activity she had so lovingly set the scene for. She explained to me that it was as if she were unable to feel Jim's touch, as if she had become insensitive to her husband's attempts to stimulate her.

The solution to Darlene's problem was to teach her how to relax and remain emotionally calm when she was in the kind of situation that usually led to intercourse. In order for her to regain the intense erotic sensations that she had experienced early in her marriage, it was necessary for her to learn to resensitize herself to her husband's touch. She eventually achieved her goal by using Creative Relaxation and a carefully graduated series of touching exercises.

STEP 1 Darlene began by practicing her Personal Quiet Time regularly twice a day. During those times she learned the basic Progressions that enabled her easily to relax each of the muscles in her body.

STEP 2 After Darlene felt comfortable doing the technique alone, she began to practice it in Jim's company. They would lie together on their bed while she experienced her Personal Quiet Time. Darlene did not move on to the next step until she could practice the technique as effectively and comfortably in her husband's presence as she could in private.

STEP 3 Darlene was asked to combine Creative Relaxation and touching, but according to strict guidelines. As preparation for this step, I reviewed some of the various ways of touching with each of them. These included techniques for varying the method, motion, and intensity of caresses. For example, I pointed out that Jim might try drawing an elongated S pattern on her body, using first his fingernails, then his fingers, and then his whole hand. Sometimes he might only brush the surface of her skin, while at other times he could rub more firmly.

Darlene and Jim were told not to undertake step 3 until evening, after dinner and when all other responsibilities were taken care of. They should then take the phone off the hook, put some favorite music on the phonograph, and have a shower together. After that, they were to nestle naked in their freshly made bed. Darlene was to practice her Personal Quiet Time while Jim gently caressed her body. Darlene, however, was told not to provide any direct stimulation for her partner. He would be the toucher, while she would remain passive. Furthermore, he was to avoid touching her genitals, and they were not to have intercourse.

After experiencing step 3, both partners made very favorable comments about it. Jim, however, was surprised—and somewhat relieved—to find that he could give Darlene pleasure by simply touching her with his hands and lips. Darlene herself found she enjoyed receiving stimulation from Jim without evaluating her response and feeling that she "had" to do something pleasurable in return.

When Darlene had shown a positive response to being touched, the couple was ready for step 4.

STEP 4 This step continued the basic strategy of step 3, except that Darlene was now free to caress Jim if she chose to. Both partners were allowed to introduce genital touching, but as in the previous step, the goal was to receive sexual pleasure from touching alone, without pressure toward intercourse or orgasm.

Again I instructed the couple in the technique of touching. For example, Jim was told to begin by touching Darlene's entire body, varying the movement patterns as in step 3 and advancing to genital touching only when he sensed (or she signaled) that she was ready for it. Even then he should progress slowly, first playing with her breasts and then with the pubic hair around her clitoris before stroking the clitoris directly. I also explained to Darlene that since a woman's sexual response is chiefly internal, she would need to let her partner know "where she was" verbally or by means of her bodily movements.

At this stage Darlene experienced the most intense erotic pleasure of her life. She felt that the touching sensations were greatly magnified and caused her great excitement and pleasure. Because she practiced Creative Relaxation as part of her therapy, both the need to evaluate herself and the anxiety and tension she had previously suffered from were eliminated. She was free to regain her lost sensitivity to touch, and once she had, she could let herself go and enjoy and participate in a complete sexual relationship.

"Our Love Is Great, but Our Sex Life Is Boring!"

Helen, an attractive young woman of thirty-three, first came to me because she was having trouble falling asleep at night. One afternoon, however, as she was being trained in Creative Relaxation, she admitted that her real problem was dissatisfaction with her sex life. She told me that throughout her married life she always had intercourse only in response to her husband's signals, moving to accommodate his erotic needs, pace, and desires. She felt tense and anxious about the situation.

Obviously, Helen needed to learn to identify and accept her own sexual needs, and to be willing to take the responsibility for achieving her own gratification. One of the major components of Creative Relaxation helped her to do this. She learned to transfer the technique of visualizing an ideal scene to sexual situations, tailoring the content of her fantasy to her own needs.

STAGE 1   I advised Helen to buy erotic literature to explore what kinds of situations and scenes stimulated her. During this period she also was trained in Creative Relaxation. In each session she practiced creating an ideal scene during her Personal Quiet Time, and I told her to continue practicing creating her own pleasing and relaxing scene between our meetings. When she came to the next training session, we discussed these scenes and her reactions to them.

STAGE 2   After her third training session, Helen was able to create vivid scenes and clearly visualize herself in them. I suggested that the next time she and her husband made love, she should experiment with creating sensuous images to accompany the experience. Because exerting conscious control over her erotic sensations had become a habit with her while she sought only to please her husband, I encouraged her to immerse herself in these images while her husband stimulated her.

STAGE 3   The boredom Helen had formerly endured during sex slowly dissolved as she took increasing responsibility for her own satisfaction by creating fantasies that suited her mood at a particular time. As it turned out, her favorite scene involved visualizing a dimly lit room, with soft music. She saw herself lying on top of a huge mound of warm mentholated shaving cream. The menthol seemed to clear her nasal passages, allowing free, uninhibited breathing, and the swirls of warm cream were luxurious to her entire body. As a result, her physical sensations and sexual pleasures were greatly enhanced.

"Don't Try So Hard—It'll Happen"

Fred was forty-eight years old, divorced, and a long-time plant manager for a large automotive company. Like Helen, he originally consulted me for a nonsexual problem. He wanted to learn how to unwind after working a full day at the plant. He finally told me, however, that he was troubled about his relationship with his girlfriend. Fred became very nervous whenever he even thought about a sexual encounter with her. She was only twenty-eight, and he was afraid that she might reject him because of his age. He feared she might prefer the younger men she had dated before she met him.

Fred's goal was to overcome the feeling that he had to prove himself to his partner during lovemaking. The anticipation of failure to perform, of course, is a great anxiety builder. In men, it often causes impotence. In Fred's case, I didn't have to lead him through a long series of therapies. One experience of using Creative Relaxation made a noticeable difference to him. I reminded Fred that he could regard his age as an asset. Because he was older, he had had experience in the finer touches of satisfying his sex partners. Furthermore, I suggested that he try to adopt an "I don't give a damn" attitude toward his performance during his next sexual encounter and use Creative Relaxation to help him relax if he began to sense symptoms of tension and anxiety.

The couple's next date began with an evening at the theater. After the show they went to Fred's apartment, where his girlfriend prepared a late dinner. Afterward, according to my instructions, Bill took her to the living room, lowered the lights, and put the same soothing music on the tape deck that he used each day when he experienced his Personal Quiet Time. Rather than lying on a couch, the couple nestled on huge, velvety-soft pillows placed on top of a thick shag carpet.

At first he gently stroked her body to enhance the overall mood. From there he was encouraged to go on with his lovemaking as he wished, being sure to keep his "I don't give a damn" attitude in mind. I had urged him to use Creative Relaxation throughout the sexual experience. For instance, whenever he started mentally to question his ability to perform, he let the thought go. In its place he visualized one of the pleasant scenes from his Personal Quiet Time. If any of his thoughts caused the familiar tightening in the chest, a queasy stomach, or a general feeling of nervousness, he practiced Creative Relaxation by concentrating on relaxing the muscles most affected by his uncomfortable thoughts.

This carefree attitude prescribed for Fred helped him reduce his tensions. It freed him from evaluating his ability to produce an adequate response. Practicing Creative Relaxation while he was in the act of making love with his girlfriend enabled him to maintain an overall calm feeling and allowed him to enjoy sex.

I saw Fred the next day. Even without any verbal communication, I knew he was very pleased with the previous evening's encounter. He commented later that by controlling his muscles through Creative Relaxation, he was also able to exercise more control over ejaculation.

"How Can I Have Pleasure without Pain?"

Mary was a middle-aged woman, happily married to her husband for over twenty-five years. However, she explained to me that she had always experienced pain during intercourse. Lately the pain seemed greater. Mary's problem is a rather common one. Gynecologists report that many of their patients complain of painful intercourse, but only in a small percentage of cases is there any structural or organic reason for it. Rather, these women are simply too tense and are therefore unable to relax their sexual muscles adequately.

Mary clearly could benefit from Creative Relaxation. As I trained her in the technique, I placed special emphasis on teaching her to recognize the different feelings associated with her muscles when they were tensed and when they were relaxed.

STAGE 1 As Mary moved through Progressions I and II, she found that she could more readily relax her muscles after contracting them if she imagined a sensation of warmth. She created this warmth by visualizing a fire burning in an old brick fireplace. She placed herself in this scene, lying on a soft rug next to the glowing fire.

STAGE 2 Once Mary had mastered the basic technique of Progressions I and II, she continued to practice them during her Personal Quiet Time. Now, however, she incorporated contracting and relaxing the muscles of her vagina, simply by adding them to the sequence of muscle groups after the buttocks muscles.

STAGE 3 By this point Mary had learned to distinguish tensed from relaxed muscles. She advanced to Progressions III and IV, in which I particularly emphasized relaxing muscles without having to contract them first. But after several practice sessions, Mary still felt that some muscle groups were more resistant than others. She eventually learned to relax them by picturing a specific muscle as a taut rubber band that would gradually contract as the tension on it was slowly reduced. She was able to use this image to help her relax the muscles of her vagina.

STAGE 4 As soon as Mary could consistently relax the muscles associated with sexuality during her Personal Quiet Time, I instructed her to transfer the same relaxed feeling to sexual encounters with her husband. Mary first successfully accomplished this transference by contracting the muscles of her vagina before attempting to relax them. As she gained more confidence, she found that she could still relax her muscles by eliminating the first step and simply imagining relaxation. Whether she tightened a muscle first or not depended on her mood at the time and on the amount of foreplay she experienced.

Mary had discovered that much of the pain she earlier suffered with intercourse had resulted from her tenseness. She said after she had completed her sessions that perhaps her tense reaction had been an attempt to deny the feelings of sexual pleasure. In any case, today she is able to experience much more enjoyment during intercourse, and her husband in turn is more easily aroused. The outcome is a mutual feeling of sexual satisfaction.

"All Systems Were Go, but Our Timing Was Off"

Bob and Susan were a young professional couple with two children and a house in the suburbs. Both complained of being overtired and too weary to enjoy a full sex life when they came home from work. After I heard the details of their typical daily routine, I was not surprised. Susan, returning from a demanding job as a nurse, immediately had to take on the roles of housekeeper, cook, and mother. After paying the baby-sitter, she went directly to the kitchen to start dinner for the family. Bob, who had just spent a hectic business day, combined the duties of yardman and father. Following dinner there were baths for the children and dishes to wash, and Bob and Susan traded off these tasks. The period remaining before the children's bedtime was devoted to family games or television viewing. After the children were tucked in, Susan did the necessary housework while Bob completed paperwork he hadn't had time to finish at the office. By eleven-thirty or so, when the couple finally crawled into bed, they were too exhausted to make love. Susan remarked, "Bob is asleep as soon as his head hits the pillow."

Naturally enough, both partners felt frustrated. While they loved each other deeply and enjoyed sex, they couldn't seem to find time for lovemaking. The solution to their problem was actually very simple. Rather than fruitlessly wish for more hours in their busy days, they learned to use Creative Relaxation to refresh and invigorate themselves so that they could take better advantage of the time already available to them.

My very first suggestion to them, however, actually had nothing directly to do with Creative Relaxation. But it did point out to them that they had become so caught up in their daily routine that they couldn't break free sufficiently to look for the common-sense answers to their problem. "Why," I asked, "don't you make love in the morning instead of late at night?" After a lengthy discussion, it finally turned out that they didn't have a lock on their bedroom door, and Susan was afraid the children would come in and interrupt them. Bob immediately installed a lock.

Then I suggested that both Bob and Susan practice their Personal Quiet Times after work. Doing this regularly would restore their energies and help them accomplish the required role switching. Bob discovered the best period for his PQT to be just before he left his office. By taking twenty minutes to practice the technique, he missed the heavy rush-hour traffic. He said he would rather sit in his office refreshing himself than in his car trying to battle his way home with all the other commuters. Susan, on the other hand, discovered that the best time for her to practice her PQT was as soon as she came home from the clinic. She made arrangements with the baby-sitter to stay an extra twenty minutes while she went upstairs to experience Creative Relaxation.

As a result of practicing their Personal Quiet Times at the end of their working days, both Bob and Susan were able to get through all of the evening domestic chores more easily, and they still had enough energy to make love when they got into bed. Furthermore, this couple soon found other ways to use Creative Relaxation to enhance their sexual relationship on their own. For example, they enjoyed practicing a Personal Quiet Time before they made love. Because both enjoyed music during their Personal Quiet Times, Bob moved the stereo into their bedroom. Listening to the music while they made love in their bed added a new and pleasurable sensation.

"Why Settle for Good When You Can Have Better?"

Virginia was a very attractive woman in her early fifties. She had been married for many years, and her children were fully grown. The youngest child had recently moved out of the family home. Some women have difficulty adjusting to the so-called empty nest, and Virginia was one of them. She didn't have enough to do during the day, and she was bored. When she took a closer look at her sexual relationship with her husband, she decided that it was boring, too. In fact, it seemed to her decidedly unsatisfactory.

When Virginia talked to me, she could clearly describe what she thought was wrong with her sex life and with her husband Michael's performance. She saw Michael as a very strong and demanding person—he was always the one to initiate sex play, and he controlled the progress toward intercourse. Even though she admitted that his lovemaking had always been pleasurable to her before, she now felt that it had become very routine and that Michael was no longer able to satisfy her.

I wondered what specifically had caused Virginia suddenly to become unhappy with a previously fairly satisfactory sexual relationship. It became evident that she was conscious of the fact that since the children had left home, she and her husband had more opportunities for sex. They didn't have to sneak around the house or wait until everyone was asleep. Rather than look at the situation as an opportunity, however, Virginia tended to view the additional time as a burden that created expectations and pressure. Sex appeared to be a chore that she mechanically performed.

The solution to Virginia's discontent was to teach her to use Creative Relaxation in order to rediscover the private self she had submerged throughout her years of motherhood and homemaking and let her learn to cherish it. As she practiced the technique, I instructed her to think of her Personal Quiet Time as a special time when she deserved quiet and rest. The twenty-minute period was an opportunity to explore who she was in addition to her various roles in life.

Virginia practiced her Personal Quiet Time faithfully twice a day, according to my instructions. She discovered that during this time her thoughts slowed down. She was able to get in touch with herself and to see more clearly the type of person she was. She realized that some of her attitudes and behavior were hurting only herself. For example, the sexual dissatisfaction she complained of was her own problem, not her husband's. Once she recognized this, she began to be responsible for determining her own sexual needs. As her confidence grew, I encouraged her to communicate these needs to Michael the next time they made love.

Let me briefly describe what Virginia explained happened:

The night was unusually romantic and the temptation to make love was overwhelming. As you looked outside from the window, all you could see was a thick blanket of freshly fallen snow, which had accumulated from the day's snowfall. The whiteness from the snow glistened and sparkled as it reflected the beam of light from the full moon. The typical Friday night sounds were muffled by the snow and by the soothing music that filled the room. My husband decided to burn one of our larger logs. Since the log was so big, the fire would burn continuously for hours. We snuggled up next to our fireplace. I could feel the warmth of my husband's body next to mine. Instead of taking my usual passive role as my husband began to touch me, I gently guided him in various ways to please me. Initially I was hesitant, mainly because I wasn't sure how my husband would respond. He willingly accepted my suggestions. Our reactions and feelings were different. I found that my husband's excitement grew as he sensed that what he was doing was extremely pleasurable to me. On the other hand, my feelings of satisfaction resulted from a combination of things. It seemed that for the first time, I was able to give myself while in the act of making love. By relaxing, I found I was able to let go and more easily communicate with my husband. After we had each climaxed, my husband surprisingly commented that he enjoyed making love because he knew that he was pleasing me and that he wasn't guessing.

As Virginia became more relaxed and accepting of herself in general, she also became more relaxed sexually, and she could accept her sexual needs as something to communicate freely to her husband. Occasionally she even made the first move toward intercourse. The outcome was a heightened feeling of mutual pleasure during sexual experiences. One of the things that stands out in Virginia's mind is that she now feels she is giving, and not simply receiving. Sex is no longer "boring" to her and she has no more complaints about the adequacy of Michael's performance. Creative Relaxation helped her gain more confidence in herself, which was reflected sexually because she was able to communicate more openly with her husband about the various ways he could please her.

As I tell the people with whom I work, Creative Relaxation is an alternative tool that you can use when you feel stress building—stress in any area of your life. You have nothing to lose by practicing it and everything to gain.

10 ❀ Coping with Life Crises

Most of us are not conditioned to accept a passive role in life. We are taught by American standards to hold ourselves responsible for what goes on in our lives. When we are confronted with situations in which we can't play an active role, frustrations mount. The stress that is created in this type of situation is referred to as "spectator stress."

Stress increases with the feeling of powerlessness. The stress that is created in a spectator varies in degree of severity. It can be something mildly irritating, such as watching your spouse embarrass himself or herself in front of strangers. It can be something as frightening as watching a member of your family lying ill in a hospital bed. Such traumas often cause people to become depressed or to escape to drinking, drugs, violence, and other forms of anti-social behavior.

In these types of situations, when no choice of yours will affect what is to happen, emotions run rampant and your energy supply is drained. It seems that you almost have to buy every physical minute, and damage is commonly your payoff. Without the practice of Creative Relaxation, these situations can cause the inexperienced to lose effectiveness and to suffer unnecessarily. Often in these situations a person is tempted to lose sight of his goals because of the intensity of the moment.

Perhaps the most severe or distressful spectator role is to witness and admit the fact that a parent or loved one is no longer capable of living independently. It is at these times that one has to learn to deal with the feelings of guilt, regret, and fear of the future. An aging parent frequently evokes these kinds of emotions. For many of us it is hard to acknowledge that our mother or father has aged. We are powerless, and the desire to bring back our parents' youth and vitality is of no avail.

Just as difficult as accepting their inability to live independently is facing the reality of approaching death. The natural tendency is to avoid these issues. The excessive stress that is created as a spectator in this role often interferes with one's ability to think clearly. Creative Relaxation helps you to face and accept reality. It assists you in gaining a perspective on the situation so that you can think more clearly. It is helpful to follow and implement each of the steps in the Pendulum Concept of stress. Identifying the stressor is sometimes difficult. The real stressor of an aging parent who is approaching death is sometimes masked by the secondary stressor of placing the parent in a nursing home facility. Additional stresses are created because families do not stay together as they once did. For the distant daughter or son, the thought of placing her or his parent in a nursing home often causes a conflict.

After doing the Personal Quiet Time and calming yourself down enough to isolate the problem, it is important that you determine what it is that you want. Once you know this, the next course of action is to determine some reasonable alternative to achieving those goals.

Paula was faced with this situation. She decided that she wanted her mother to have security and the best care. She wanted the responsibility fulfilled without having it disrupt her own household. Since Paula's mother was all alone, her first idea was to have her mother come and live with them. Once she objectively considered what it would entail, Paula realized that she wanted her mother to live with her to satisfy her own feelings of guilt. It would mean that her mother would have to move from New York to Michigan, where she had no friends. During the day, her mother would be left alone, because the kids went to school and Paula and her husband worked. She would be home without any transportation and without help, if needed.

Paula and her husband decided that the only way to provide her mother with optimal care and comfort was to place her in a nursing home. They agreed to visit her frequently and to call once a week to say hello and to share any news.

Once you have considered as many reasonable alternatives as possible, select the one that contributes most toward reaching your goal, and then take action. A lot of stress can be saved by planning what you can do and accepting what you can't do. You can bring the skills that you have learned from Creative Relaxation to help you to bear and resolve this kind of stressful situation.

Another client, Don, found great value in Creative Relaxation skills when his oldest child, a senior in high school, told him that she did not want to go to college. This is an example of spectator stress, because the decision ultimately belonged to Don's daughter. The father's dreams of seeing his daughter succeed in life and have numerous opportunities was suddenly shattered. The frustration built up as

Don began to fabricate in his mind a web of worries by continuously asking himself questions like "What if my daughter isn't able to get the job she wants later in life because she doesn't have a college degree?" or "What if she gets a job and starts working after graduating from high school? How will she find a suitable husband?" At times he is frightened by his own thoughts when he starts asking himself what he would do if some of his thoughts came true.

Creative Relaxation helped Don to unwind enough to see what he was doing to himself and the other family members. He stopped thinking the fearful thoughts by reaffirming that his daughter was no longer a child and that it was her life to live. He resolved in his mind that she needed to make up her own mind. In order for Don to feel more comfortable, he needed to share with his daughter his thoughts and reservations. He pointed out that he had the money to pay for her college education. He also felt that it was important to be supportive and not to let his love for his daughter be affected by her choice.

Whenever he would get worried, he would negate the negative stress and would replay in his mind the important conclusions he had reached. At times, when all of the stress seemed to compound itself and he started feeling sorry for himself, he would grant himself seven minutes to do all the complaining about his daughter he wanted and to allow his sorrows to emerge freely. At the end of the seven minutes, he had to get his thoughts together and take the next step.

The increased patience (combined with the ability to think rationally) that results from Creative Relaxation was helpful to another parent, whose son is a dirt bike enthusiast. Laura was fearful for her son's safety every time he left the house to ride the dirt bike. On days when she heard a siren, she got an earache because she was trying to listen for her son to come home. She didn't relax from the time he left until the time he walked in the front door. There were days when she nagged her son about everything he did around the house. She was, in a sense, punishing him for the time she felt he punished her.

As a result of learning and practicing Creative Relaxation, Laura learned to associate certain reactions with the fear she had of her son's riding the bike. Whenever she felt the reactions, she would do the technique. It would lower her stress level and help her to realize that her nagging was her way of paying him back for all the suffering he caused her.

Much of Laura's stress was created as a spectator. She felt helpless when her son was out riding his bike. She decided that all her worrying was affecting only herself. She decided that she needed to get herself involved in projects that would occupy her mind and keep her physically active. She practiced talking to herself when her son was out on his bike, to help her to focus on her own goals and her son's goals. Furthermore, she developed a plan that encouraged doing other things with her son to enhance their relationship instead of nagging him about his bike.

Situations that do not have lifelong implications are nevertheless origins of stress for people in spectator roles. For example, suppose your husband's mother does not approve of the way you keep house. Frequently a mother-in-law cannot accept a passive role as a spectator. You end up being the spectator, feeling helpless during an in-law's visit, because you know her stay is limited and you don't want to start family troubles. Nevertheless, your stress level easily rises when your in-law starts complaining about all the cobwebs she found in the house. Or she may question how you could let the windows go uncleaned for so long. The cluttered linen closet and the dirty lampshades are next on her list of things to comment about. Often the real stress raiser appears when you go to find something in the kitchen and it is not there, and you have to go to your mother-in-law to find out where your kitchen utensils "belong."

Later in marriage the spectator role may change as children enter the picture. The stress climbs as your in-laws interfere with raising your children. In a matter of a few days you hear your mother-in-law pointing out to the children your cruelty for not letting them eat that little bit of candy or for making them go to bed so early. Each time, you feel the frustration mounting.

A similar situation exists when a member of your family comes to live with you. One couple had agreed to let the wife's youngest sister live with them. Her mother was having difficulty disciplining her, and everyone felt that it would help to have Carol move in with her older sister, Karen. In no time, Karen felt herself in a spectator's role. Carol would not cooperate. She would leave the house without letting anyone know where she was going or when she would return. Her room was always a mess. When she was home she would tie up the phone for hours. Karen was caught in the middle. When their mother phoned, Karen would get criticized for not taking better care of her sister.

Karen did practice Creative Relaxation to help her deal with everyday frustrations. By calming down, it became evident to Karen that the situation had to be changed. She sat down with her husband and together they devised a list that included everything that was expected of Carol. Their plan was that if Carol was not willing to comply and follow through with the items on the list, then she needed to make other plans. In this situation, Creative Relaxation helped Karen to manufacture enough strength to follow through with her plans.

A tough role for any spouse involves watching his or her mate quickly age because of job pressures. More commonly it is the wife who is placed in the spectator's role, watching her husband come home night after night with problems from the office. When he walks in the door, he has a stern look on his face and his forehead is wrinkled from all of the frustrations of the day. When his wife tries to tell him not to worry, it does no good, because deep down he loves his work. The real difficulty for the spectator in this case is to learn to accept the situation. A wife may feel helpless because she knows that even if she tried to change her husband, he is not going to change. Nonetheless, she sees him deteriorating and fears for his health. Creative Relaxation is helpful to the spectator in this role because it helps her to realize that the other person's life is his own responsibility.

One woman faced with this situation decided to share her concerns with her husband. She knew he was deeply dedicated to his work as a police officer. She also knew that it would be unfair to ask him to leave the force. Their conversations displayed a deep concern for each other. The feelings that were generated were warm and tender. The officer's wife was surprised to learn that he, too, felt victimized and helpless in his role. He was aware of the toll that his work was taking on his health. He realized that after he had served fifteen years on the force, the work was affecting his health. But it was part of him and he loved it.

Now in his forties, he was frightened by the thought of changing careers. He even questioned his ability to learn another skill—which in any case would be too risky because he had numerous financial responsibilities to fulfill. Another important consideration was that in a few years he would be eligible for retirement. At that time he would receive a good pension and fringe benefits. So for him, to leave the police force seemed impossible. His only choice was to endure the time remaining until he could retire.

Since her husband was not willing to give up a career, the wife had to learn to accept him as he was and to understand that even though his work was demanding, it was a part of him and brought him some happiness, which contributed positively to their marriage. Creative Relaxation helped the wife to control her worry and to realize that the best way to show her love was to be supportive and to channel her energies into building a good marriage. When the frustrations of life seemed complex, this couple was able to pull themselves together long enough to realize that they had each other and that was a primary goal that they both wanted to maintain.

But spectator stress does not arise only in very serious situations. More frequently we encounter the frustrations of a spectator during everyday occurrences. In some daily situations you will find that your options for coping vary. You may be standing around waiting to purchase something in a store, with no salesperson nearby to help you. One woman said that when that happens to her, she goes crazy. She remembered one time when she went to the gift department of a large store to find a present for a friend. She was pressed for time. As soon as she entered the department someone immediately approached her to see if she needed any assistance in finding a gift. However, when it came time to pay for the merchandise, no salesperson was available. After she had waited several minutes, a saleswoman appeared. Just as the saleswoman was about to help her, the phone rang. As the only employee available, she had to answer the phone. The minutes ticked away as the woman stood there helplessly waiting for this salesperson to finish talking to the customer on the phone. Meanwhile, her stress level continued to rise.

If a similar situation occurs to you, try to become aware of any negative stress reactions and immediately negate them as soon as they are identified. This can be done by using any one of the methods previously suggested. Next, redetermine what you want. At the same time, consider your alternatives. For instance, one alternative would be to put the product back on the shelf and go back for it another time. Another alternative would be to go to the customer complaint department and suggest that they add additional people on the floor to help answer phone calls.

If you elect to stand there and wait, try to imagine the person responsible for the phone call or delay as being old or sick, lying on a couch at home, without transportation and needing assistance. Visualizing this kind of picture creates sympathy and at the same time helps to control your stress level. The important thing is to conserve your supply of adaptive energy, which is often wasted in a spectator's role.

A similar situation involves standing on a golf course holding your tongue while a friend lines up poorly for his golf shot. The stress inside you rises as you stand there knowing the consequences of what is ahead. Your first impulse is to point it out to your friend before he is about to hit the ball. Yet how many of us can recall disliking a school subject, a sport, or a particular career because someone kept pointing out our mistakes? Some people, in the course of trying to tell you how to improve in a particular area, also tell you how bad you are. Being told the right way is not always the best way to learn.

When you are a spectator in these kinds of situations, use Creative Relaxation to help you think more clearly, stay unemotional, and objectively evaluate the situation. For instance, you should consider if the timing is appropriate. Many golfers resent being coached on the golf course. They believe that you play golf on the golf course and you practice and work on your swing on the driving range.

You also need to know exactly what you want to say. Even if your eye is sharp for pointing out errors, do you know what to tell your friend to help him? Another consideration is to determine if he is receptive to criticism. Most important, you must give your friends helpful advice that they can handle. Some people have a natural gift for giving criticism; most people, unfortunately, do not.

The spectator stress rises easily when you are faced with situations in which your options are more limited. For instance, most of us have experienced waiting for the doctor in an examining room, fully undressed. You sit there helplessly, while the doctor takes his time getting to you. You would get dressed and leave, but if you want to have your examination, then you are at the mercy of your doctor.

A similar situation that many of us women can relate to is going to a beauty shop and having to wait to get our hair cut. After your hair has been washed, you sit in a chair with a towel wrapped around your head as you wait for your turn. Again, you have the option to leave, but it is rather difficult to walk out with a wet head of hair, especially if you have another appointment scheduled afterward.

When traveling by airplane, many people have the unpleasant experience of arriving at their destination as scheduled, only to find out their luggage did not arrive with them. When this happens, your options are limited. Sometimes you can wait for the next flight and hope that your luggage is on board. Or you can request to have your luggage delivered to your location when it arrives. In the meantime, you are left without any of your belongings or a change of clothes. If you feel really desperate, you can usually replace some of your essential items.

The common tendency in these types of spectator-stress situations is to take your frustrations out on an innocent bystander—often someone whom you feel very deeply about. When this occurs, the innocent bystander ends up being placed in a spectator's role and becomes another victim of the circumstances. Creative Relaxation helps you to negate the negative stress that is produced in these instances and enables you to think more clearly so you can consider your alternatives and make the wisest choice. The technique is also valuable in helping you cope with situations where you are completely at the mercy of elements such as weather, other people, or material things.

For example, you have scheduled brochures or Christmas cards to arrive at a certain date, but because of delays due to weather or the postal system itself, the mail doesn't get delivered on time. Another such situation arises when you go to a football game and you park your car in a huge lot with 50,000 other cars. Before the end of the game, you dash out of the stadium to beat the traffic, only to find your car blocked by that of someone else who is still up in the stands watching the end of the game.

Patience is a virtue in these kinds of stressful situations. Creative Relaxation enables you to maintain patience. At the same time, it helps you to cope rationally and develop reasonable alternatives.

During a training session, one woman who had been successfully integrating Creative Relaxation into her life-style commented about one unusual situation in which all the Creative Relaxation in the world would not have helped. She had been invited to an important business party. Specifically for this event, she bought a luxurious cocktail dress. Rather than buy a new pair of shoes, she decided to have an older pair redone at a shoe repair shop that was located in the lobby of her apartment building. Her previous experiences with this shoe store were positive, and she felt their work was reliable.

On the day of the party she stopped off at the shoe store after work to pick up her shoes, never thinking to check the contents of the bag before leaving the shop. As she was getting dressed she opened the bag to get her shoes. Something looked different about the shoes, even though the color and style looked the same. As she went to put the shoes on, she realized that the shoes were too small. Rather than wear another outfit for which she had shoes to match, she stubbornly decided to wear the shoes that were not hers to the party. Later that evening, the pain in her feet was excruciating. She said that at that moment, practicing Creative Relaxation wouldn't help. She decided that the only thing that would help her feet was to take off her shoes and go barefoot the rest of the night.

As she told the whole incident, she never mentioned feeling angry or upset. As a matter of fact, she thought that the whole situation was rather humorous as she labeled herself a victim of spectator's stress. I quickly pointed out that she was in fact an effective user of spectator stress!

11 ❀ Winning at Sports

Some of the most exciting and memorable times in my life were my nine years of competition in platform and spring board diving. I learned that competition in sports is more than aiming to win a gold medal.

Early in his or her career, an athlete learns what it means to stay in there and keep trying. In moments of extreme pressure, a seasoned athlete is able to rely on his physical and mental strengths and coordinate them in such a way that it mobilizes him to victory. It takes many years for an athlete to develop the mental qualities of a champion. The mental training that I received began early in my career. One saying that I carried with me throughout my diving career (and continue to rely on to this day) came from a swimming coach who trained the Olympic team back in the 1940s. During practice one day he told me always to remember that "I am as good as the best, and better than the rest." From that day, I realized that competition involved learning how to compete first with myself.

Competing with yourself means learning how to set realistic goals. It means developing a belief in yourself and not giving up, even when things get tough. One of the toughest situations that I can recall occurred early in my career when I competed at my first national championship meet. Besides being my first national meet, it was also the farthest I had ever traveled to dive. For the three-meter competition, I was positioned to dive after the previous year's national champion. It is hard to describe the feeling of waiting for one's turn at the back of the diving board and for the first time hearing crowds of people cheering and applauding for the near-perfect dive that the national champion just performed. The situation grew more intense when my name was announced and the crowds suddenly became silent out of politeness. As I stood on the board ready to dive, I felt all of three feet tall. It was at that moment that I learned the significance of thinking of yourself as being as good as the best and better than the rest.

An experienced athlete who has learned how to compete with himself knows how to convert that same situation into a challenge. He is able to maintain his composure and direct his energies positively in order to do the job. Other athletes choose to compete against other people. This can be positive, if an athlete uses this as an extra source of motivation—as in track, for instance, when on the final lap of a race you decide to extend yourself beyond your physical limits to beat the person in front of you. Competition against others can have a negative effect if it causes you to give up your strategy or if you lose sight of your goals. For example, a runner may lose a race at the finish line because he turned his head to the side to see where he was in relationship to the competition.

It is during those self-defeating times that an athlete benefits most from learning how to think positively. The use of imagery was another helpful skill that I received training in late in my diving career. Even though I never had the opportunity to use and benefit from Creative Relaxation with my diving, other athletes are finding it helpful.

Practicing the technique does not make an athlete something he is not. Creative Relaxation helps to rechannel or lower, if necessary, your stress level so that your ability to perform is not interfered with. Everyone knows that when an athlete feels tense and uptight, his or her performance ability decreases. A muscle that is already tensed because of nervousness, fear, or anxieties does not contract with maximal force. The quality of movement is also interfered with when muscles are continuously tense. Free-flowing movement that requires minimal energy expenditure is created when antagonist muscles appropriately relax. Frequently injuries occur when the opposing muscle is tightened.

Learning when to contract a specific muscle to execute a move is a skill. Inexperienced skaters are frequently disillusioned about the amount of skill required to make certain moves after watching the grace and ease of Peggy Fleming's style of skating. People walk away thinking how easy it is. As soon as they put on a pair of skates and get on the ice, they are quick to realize the enormous amount of skill required. Peggy Fleming has learned over the years how to use only those muscles necessary to execute a particular move. She knows when and where to relax certain muscles and tense others.

Creative Relaxation enables one to relax specific muscles in the body that interfere with the desired movement.

At the same time, it increases the forcefulness of contraction from the various muscles that are needed to complete the movement.

You can relax the muscles in your body simply by following the suggestions presented earlier in this book. When should you negate the negative stress reactions? That is really up to you. Keep in mind that what you really want is to maximize your performance. If you focus on that, then the best time to negate any negative stress reactions will be determined when you find your performance enhanced. Many people find it most beneficial to relax the body before they begin to execute a move.

Creative Relaxation helps an athlete to deal better with feelings of self-doubt. If you begin doubting yourself and cluttering your mind with all sorts of negative thoughts before and during the competition, let go of those thoughts by integrating the training that you learned from practicing the Personal Quiet Time.

Treat your negative thought as "just another thought." As soon as you recognize that you are thinking a negative thought, simply let it go and return your attention to what you are doing. Don't give too much importance to the fact that you were thinking a negative thought. It's no big deal. Some people find it easier to let go of the negative thought by mentally picturing the thought as a sentence. Once the sentence is clearly fixed in their mind, they imagine it being crossed out with a huge X and then simply discard it.

Sometimes a negative thought can be removed by replacing it with a positive one. As soon as you remove the negative thought, negate any other noticeable negative stress reactions that occurred as a natural response to the negative thought.

Creative Relaxation is also a useful tool with imagery training. Many athletes are encouraged by their coaches to use imagery by visualizing themselves executing the perfect skill. For effective use of imagery, one must be totally relaxed. When the body is at ease physically, emotionally, and mentally, the mind is not cluttered with interfering thoughts, but is free to visualize a clear picture that will create the sensation that the event is happening for real.

Creative Relaxation is helpful with imagery training because it teaches, through each of the five Progressions in the Personal Quiet Time, how to create a pleasant scene. You also gain experience in mentally picturing yourself in the scene. Throughout the exercise you are relating to the scene and are using it to stimulate the relaxed feelings.

Athletes can create a clearer mental picture of themselves performing by practicing in front of a mirror, looking at their own pictures, or viewing a videotape recording. The more an athlete relaxes and the more closely the mental picture resembles the actual situation, the sooner the athlete makes the desired change.

Greg is an example of a young collegiate diver who learned to combine imagery and Creative Relaxation to help himself more quickly break a habit of leaning forward on his front three-and-a-half somersault. Each day at the end of the Personal Quiet Time, he would visualize himself executing the dive correctly. After mentally practicing the dive for about two weeks, he started standing up straight on his take-off.

Creative Relaxation also assists in sports by increasing one's ability to concentrate. Frequently when an athlete's stress level rises above the optimal level, or when his stress is misdirected, concentration is interfered with. One professional football player found it difficult to concentrate on the playing field whenever he had to sit on the bench for a long period of time. Negative stress was created because he had difficulty accepting that the only time he could play was when the coach called him into the game. When the coach did call him into the game, additional pressures resulted because he was expected to perform after sitting for such a long time. At other times the excitement from the crowds interfered with his ability to concentrate and get the job done. As he ran down the field to catch a pass, he could hear the screams of the crowd. At the crucial point when his arms were reaching for the ball, the noise from the crowd would divert his attention momentarily, causing the ball to slip through his fingers.

Training in Creative Relaxation helped this player to concentrate on his game. Between the scheduled practice sessions, he would sit down for a Personal Quiet Time. At the end of the session, he would picture himself playing in a game in his team's home field: It's the fourth quarter and the score is tied. Only a few minutes remain on the clock. The people in the stands are on their feet with excitement. Their team has the ball. The team is lined up in a pass formation. The ball is snapped. The player hurtles downfield to receive the pass. At the same time, he feels his muscles straining as his heart and lungs coordinate their working efforts in order to provide the muscles with enough oxygen. His mind is totally occupied with the thought of catching the football. The noises from the crowd are muffled in the background as his ears are tuned in to the sounds of the other players approaching. Even though the pressure is great, his body feels relaxed as he confidently extends his arms and catches the football.

Repeatedly he would review this play in his mind. When he was in a real game situation, he found that his body knew what to do.

Athletes frequently lose their ability to concentrate when they get cold. For many athletes, the peak time for getting cold is just before a competitive event. Often the coldness is a reaction to the pressures and fears of the meet. Nancy is a young swimmer who complained of always being cold just before she was to swim. All of her attention focused on being cold instead of on how she was going to swim the event.

After going through the program in Creative Relaxation, she realized that much of her coldness was related to her fear of failure. She used the coldness as an excuse to justify her losing. I explained to her that by letting herself get cold, she was making it more likely that she would lose. Besides interfering with her concentration, getting cold was causing her muscles to tense up and slowing her down.

Now Nancy uses Creative Relaxation to help her cope better when she does lose. She also practices the technique to help her stay warm, and this helps her performance. During a meet she wraps up in a large beach towel and mentally envisions warm, bright sunlight penetrating her body and relaxing her muscles.

It is important to keep in mind that athletic competition is just that—it is athletics. When you start to think of athletics as the measure of your character rather than of the quality of a physical performance on a given day, then your goals have been lost or exaggerated. It is time to re-evaluate your list of goals and ask yourself what you really want, and why.

Many people enjoy participating in noncompetitive sport activities such as jogging and bicycling. For some, these leisure sports are a way of getting exercise and maintaining health, or of losing weight. Others enjoy leisure sports as social occasions or because they are opportunities to get away from all the pressures and worries at work.

Whatever your reason for participating in leisure sports, you will find Creative Relaxation helpful in this area, too. The application and potential benefit of Creative Relaxation in leisure sports is occasionally the motivating factor for a person to undergo training in the technique, as in the case of Joe and Janet.

The couple was advised by their doctor to get training in Creative Relaxation. Joe rationalized that he did not need any training, even though he suffered from high blood pressure and frequently had difficulty falling asleep at night. Janet eagerly underwent training. After she had practiced Creative Relaxation for three weeks, Janet's long-standing stomach pain went away. To her husband's amazement, her bowling average increased. She attributed her bowling success to Creative Relaxation. She benefits by using the technique to help her relax before she starts her approach. Standing in the ready position with her ball comfortably positioned in her hands, she inhales deeply and smoothly. She holds momentarily, before she exhales, and relaxes her muscles. Janet says that the relaxed feeling enables her to execute her swing more smoothly. She says that it is like bowling to mental music. Her husband is impressed with his wife's overall improvement. He suddenly feels that he can benefit from learning Creative Relaxation.

Another person who was an avid bowler was not too enthusiastic about Creative Relaxation at the onset of the five-week training program until he discovered that the technique helped him improve his bowling score. Each week Lou would get together with several fellow workers and go bowling. One of those evenings he bowled a terrible first game. Being the athlete that he was, Lou was furious with himself. Each time he saw the low score on the score sheet, it angered him even more. Before he started to bowl his second game, he happened to think of trying Creative Relaxation. To his relief, he bowled a fabulous second game. He benefited by using the technique to help him relax before his turn. He found that it was easier for him to concentrate on what he wanted to do. The noises and the different people moving around did not distract him as they had before. He was so excited after his high-scoring second game—that he blew his third game!

That evening Lou realized the skill involved in the technique. He also discovered that Creative Relaxation could be of benefit to him in a variety of situations and that its use was not limited solely to bad times.

Creative Relaxation can even be of benefit when you are playing cards. In certain card games, such as blackjack, five-card stud, hearts, and bridge, a deadpan expression is essential. Sometimes it is difficult to keep a straight face, especially when you are holding a fantastic hand or when you are trying to get by with a bluff. Creative Relaxation enables you to negate any negative stress reactions that might cause you to give away your hand to the other players. Not only are you sensitive to your own stress signals, but you are also more sensitive to the other players around you.

One person who enjoyed playing cards learned to recognize when a player friend of his was bluffing. He noticed that his friend would forcefully try to relax when he was trying to deceive him. He also recognized that his friend's movements were jerky and sharp. His newly acquired stress awareness helped to increase his winnings.

By now you can see how Creative Relaxation can easily be applied to bridge. Many people are falsely led into believing that they are coming over to someone's house to "play" bridge. At some point the game suddenly changes from a social activity to an effort to "win at all costs." The person making the shift becomes irate, hostile, and angry at everyone at the table, including his or her partner.

Dancing is another leisure activity in which Creative Relaxation is helpful. A young woman named Pat was given a birthday party by her relatives and close friends.

Throughout the evening she reluctantly accepted any offers to dance. She felt obligated to dance because the party was for her. Each time she danced, she felt awkward, as her body was tense and moved very rigidly. During a slow dance, Pat was being led on the dance floor by a magnificent dancer. While they were dancing together, he quietly told Pat to try to relax. Rather than being offended, she considered it a challenge because it reminded her that she could use the skills she had learned from Creative Relaxation to help her relax.

Without missing a step, she negated the negative stress reactions, inhaling smoothly and exhaling slowly and completely. As she exhaled, she attempted to capture the calm and relaxed feelings that she felt during her Personal Quiet Time. She repeated this a couple of times. Almost immediately, she found herself moving more freely with her partner as he expertly led her across the floor. When the music stopped, Pat was pleased with herself. For the rest of the evening she looked forward to other opportunities to dance.

Creative Relaxation is helpful in sports where precision and split-second timing are crucial. In golf, for example, timing and accuracy are crucial to the player's success. A common problem of golfers is that they bring their hands down too quickly at the top of the backswing. This causes them to rush a shot and lose distance on the ball because the ball is hit mostly with their arms and not their body. One golfer learned to overcome this habit by using Creative Relaxation at the top of his backswing. Once he brought his club back to the top of his backswing, he would briefly pause to create a momentary feeling of being relaxed before bringing the club down to hit the ball. He found that creating that instant flash of relaxation was just enough time to allow his body and hips to get into the shot. He drove the ball farther each time and, to his delight, lowered his golf score.

Another golfer benefited from Creative Relaxation to help him keep his head down when he swung at the ball. He had the habit of picking his head up too soon, in anticipation of looking for his ball. When he lifted his head too quickly, the ball would veer off to the right. He learned to keep his head down by relaxing his body each time he addressed the ball. He would think, "Relax" as he inhaled and exhaled smoothly and evenly before starting his swing. After hitting the ball he would again think, "Relax." Simultaneously, he would focus his attention on the spot where the ball was lying on the ground. Occasionally when he felt anxious and tempted to lift his head, he would ask another golfer to watch his shot. This also helped him to lower his stress level and improve his game.

Tennis is another sport in which precision and timing are important. Beginning players frequently panic when they are expected to return a ball that is served too fast. Sally used to freeze whenever a serve came at her too fast. Through Creative Relaxation, she learned to eliminate several stress reactions that she made before returning the serve, such as tightly gripping the handle of the racket or rocking back and forth on her feet. Sally found that she was not as startled and afraid of the oncoming ball if she told herself to relax and pictured her body in a state of readiness.

Joggers can benefit from using Creative Relaxation, too. Charles discovered that while running he would needlessly tighten the muscles in his jaw and shoulders and clench his fists. Now when he runs, he relaxes the various muscles in his body that are not necessary for propelling him forward. He finds that he runs more smoothly and is less tired at the end of his run. Other joggers have found that the increased body awareness that they gain from practicing

Creative Relaxation helps them to stay attuned to the various signals being emitted from their bodies when they run. This increased awareness helps to reduce the number of athletic injuries that may occur when an athlete pushes himself beyond his limits.

Some joggers use Creative Relaxation to help them maintain a smooth breathing pattern. Joggers report that they run more rhythmically and easily when their breathing is smooth and regular. It is recommended that you try inhaling quickly for two counts, then exhaling more slowly and evenly for four counts.

Lap swimmers also find that breathing in this rhythmical pattern helps them to maintain an even cadence. They claim that they don't work so hard when they are swimming, and at the end, like the joggers, they are not as tired. One swimmer learned how to regulate this smooth breathing pattern by blowing bubbles when she swam. She found that the breast stroke was the easiest stroke to begin with in learning how to breathe rhythmically. Swimming the breast stroke afforded her the opportunity to blow bubbles comfortably out of her mouth as she exhaled for four counts. Blowing the bubbles through her mouth helped her develop a rhythmical pattern of breathing. It regulated the exhaling so that it was smoother and slower. Each time, she practiced exhaling for four counts and inhaling for two counts. Once she learned how to master the rhythmical pattern of breathing with the breast stroke, she found it simple to transfer it to the other strokes. She commented that, if nothing else, concentrating on her breathing helped to break up the boredom of swimming laps.

People who enjoy participating in an exercise program at a health club or an exercise class have found that the Creative Relaxation technique enables them to be more flexible during various stretching exercises. For instance, during the toe-touching exercise, one woman is able to touch her toes more easily by using Creative Relaxation to relax the muscles in the backs of her legs. When she starts bending down at her waist to touch her toes with her fingertips, she imagines that the backs of her legs are being massaged, and she pictures the muscles giving in as they lengthen. Since she has started using Creative Relaxation in combination with her exercise program, she has found that she is more flexible and the next day experiences less pain and soreness.

Don't forget that practicing Creative Relaxation in competitive or leisure sports will not make you something you're not. What it will do is eliminate the tension and anxiety that interfere with the performance of whatever skills you have learned, and thus add to your fulfillment. Moreover, you will get the most out of the technique when you make it an integral part of the Basic Four: proper diet, exercise, adequate sleep, and Creative Relaxation. This is what winning the stress game is all about.

12 ✿ Conclusion

Up to this point the main focus of this book has been on what you ought to be doing. Let's stop and take a moment to look at what you actually are doing.

Answer the questionnaire "How Do I Treat Myself?" If, after filling it out, you discover that your score is above 34 points, then you can benefit from reading this chapter and learning how to treat yourself more kindly.

How Do I Treat Myself?

DIRECTIONS: For each of the following questions, circle the number that comes closest to expressing your usual daily experience. 1 = Seldom; 2 = Sometimes; 3 = Almost Always. These are only your opinions, so there are no "right" or "wrong" answers. When you have completed the questionnaire, add up the numbers you circled to get your score.

1. Do you skip breakfast in the morning in order to sleep longer because you have a long day ahead?   1   2   3

2. Do you come home after work and have a beer or cocktail to unwind?   1 2 3

3. Do you eat standing up?   1 2 3

4. Do you finish your meals in about fifteen minutes?   1 2 3

5. Do you wait until you are in serious pain before you seek professional help?   1 2 3

6. Do you have certain employees who upset you?   1 2 3

7. Do you find it difficult to enjoy yourself and relax when you are away from work?   1 2 3

8. Do you watch TV and think about or do several other things at the same time?   1 2 3

9. Do you postpone studying for an exam or completing a project until it becomes a crisis?   1 2 3

10. When things are going smoothly, do you begin to look for a problem or a small issue and make it a big issue?   1 2 3

11. When in a conversation with another person, do you find yourself thinking about other things?   1 2 3

12. Do you try to squeeze in extra projects before you are to leave for an appointment?   1 2 3

13. Do you put off doing tasks you dislike?   1 2 3

14. Do you find yourself forgetting things and having to retrace your steps?   1 2 3

15. Do you take on responsibilities that are really not your own?   1 2 3

16. Do you skip meals in order to accomplish more things in a day?   1   2   3

17. Do you feel uncomfortable or that you are not being productive when you sit down to read a book, watch TV, or read a newspaper?   1   2   3

18. Do you worry about making money stretch, losing a job, a child's illness, or troubles with your spouse?   1   2   3

19. Do you let a bad morning ruin your day?   1   2   3

20. Do you eat and read at the same time?   1   2   3

21. Do you have difficulties falling asleep the night before an important meeting or event?   1   2   3

22. When you are spending time with your children, are you thinking of things that need to be done at work?   1   2   3

23. Do you take vitamins or go on weight-reducing diets without consulting your physician?   1   2   3

Responding "Sometimes" or "Almost Always" to questions 1, 3, 4, or 16 means that an extra stress is added to your body.

It is not a good idea to eat and read at the same time because you may tend to overeat. When you are absorbed in your reading, you tend not to pay attention to the signals from your body that are telling you that you are full. As a result, you may eat too much. Additional stress is created if you are trying to lose weight.

The habit of eating too quickly might best be explained with the Stress Momentum concept. At one point in your life, conditions may have been such that it was necessary for you to eat rapidly. For instance, maybe you grew up in a family where everyone had big appetites and ate very quickly. So, in order for you to get enough food to eat, you had to eat quickly, too. Over a period of time, conditions change. You may no longer eat with your family, yet continue to eat quickly. Eating quickly no longer serves any purpose, but it has become a habit. Eating too quickly is a strain on your body's digestive system. Eating more slowly aids digestion because it makes it easier for the digestive juices to break down and extract the various nutrients and minerals from the food.

Skipping a meal can be more or less stressful, depending upon whether you are skipping the meal because you want to or because you do not have enough time. More stress is added when you want to eat but your schedule won't permit it. If this is your situation, then you could benefit from looking at how you organize and manage your day.

If you examine questions 9, 10, and 12, you will see that they refer to stress-producing situations that you may be creating for yourself. Squeezing extra projects into a limited amount of time is playing what I have called "Beat the Clock." Players of the game claim that it is an exciting way to motivate themselves and add extra pressure to their day. The odds of losing at this game are high and the consequences costly. It is not uncommon for losers to suffer from arguments, retracing steps, anxiety, headaches, and sleepless nights. Long-term players of the game frequently suffer from ulcers, upset stomachs, and high blood pressure. Being aware of when you are playing the game and remembering to focus on the priorities you want to accomplish are essential to victory in this game—as long as you continue to play.

Putting off a task is not considered the most effective way

to use your supply of adaptive energy, because of all the mental stress you go through. At the same time, taking on problems that are not yours clearly uses more of your adaptive energy because you are adding more stresses to your life. Knowing your optimal stress level and being able to say no are important to maintaining your ability to be effective.

Answering the following questions with a 3 are early warning signs of mischanneling stress: 2, 7, 8, 14, 17, 21, 22. These questions highlight your reactions to various situations. Even though some of these reactions will add stress, they are mainly indicators of mischanneling stress. They are motivators for you to begin looking for ways to more positively channel stress.

The challenge is, what are you going to do about this misdirected stress? One suggestion is to sit or lie down and practice the Personal Quiet Time, and afterward, before getting up, decide what you want to do the rest of the day or night.

We each expect ourselves to function optimally, yet many of us don't treat ourselves that way. It is my belief that many of us take better care of our automobiles than we do of ourselves. Driving around in a dirty car is unacceptable to many people. We spend a lot of time and money to make sure that the outside and inside of our cars are presentable. We do the same thing with our bodies. Huge sums of money are spent each year to buy makeup, perfumes, fashionable clothes, and shoes, and to have our hair cut and styled. But what about the inner mechanisms—what do we do for those?

Many car owners insist on putting only the highest grade of gasoline in their cars. When you ask them why, they simply reply that it enables the car to run more smoothly.

Those are usually the same people who use the best type of oil for their cars and have regular oil changes. As soon as the car sounds as if it is missing, or after so many miles, without hesitating, people will take the car to the garage for a tune-up or will do it themselves. How many of you treat your inner "machinery" as well as you treat your car? Are the foods you eat each day equivalent in quality to the gas and oil that you put into your car? Do you regularly give your body a tune-up?

Some people say that they regularly go to their doctor for a physical examination. That is important and should be continued. However, a physical examination is a check-up, not a tune-up. The Creative Relaxation technique is one way to give your body a daily tune-up. A great number of us take our health for granted. It is only when we lose it that we realize how important it really is. Creative Relaxation alone is not enough for maintaining optimal health. Winning at the stress game plus having quality health involves incorporating into your life the Basic Four. Just as there are the four food groups basic to good nutrition, there are four groups basic to optimal health. The Basic Four are getting adequate sleep, eating a proper diet, exercising regularly, and practicing Creative Relaxation daily.

Practitioners of Creative Relaxation have learned how to control their diets by using Creative Relaxation. You can put on the pounds when you get the munchies or, as one woman described, a case of motor-mouth. If you have motor-mouth syndrome, you can't stop eating. The momentum begins as soon as you put something into your mouth. Then you blaze through the kitchen, eating everything in sight. One weekend sufferer has learned to recognize that before she makes her way to the refrigerator she feels an excited sensation mounting inside her. She also notices that her chest tightens and her breathing becomes irregular in anticipation of looking at food. The outcome is an uncontrollable desire to consume food.

She learned to integrate Creative Relaxation to reduce her cravings. Now, when she approaches the refrigerator on the weekends, she negates the tightening sensations in her chest by practicing the methods described earlier in this book. This helps her to stop herself long enough to ask herself two important questions: (1) Am I hungry? and (2) Are a few minutes of eating worth the effort needed to get the extra pounds off?

As soon as she calms herself, she realizes how worthless her eating spree would be because in a few minutes all the food would be eaten and she would be in the same predicament as before. Also, she stops to think about the short time and little effort it takes for her to ingest the food as opposed to the arduous task of burning off the extra calories. When she does begin to eat, she has found that she still can gain control over herself. Before, once she got started she would say to herself something like "Well, I blew it. What difference does it make now?" as she continued to haul in the food. Now she is able to slow herself enough through Creative Relaxation to stop the eating before she has done a lot of damage.

One woman stopped her food cravings by putting a sign on her refrigerator door that said, "Stop and relax." This helped her to become aware of her present stress level, to negate any anxious feelings, and to stop.

A college student lost five pounds by practicing the Personal Quiet Time instead of eating when she had such cravings. Another person learned to handle the excited feelings after negating the stress by asking himself, "Who is in control? The food or me?"

Weight-conscious people have invariably been told to

avoid between-meal nibbling by finding something else to do. One woman expanded and modified this idea to make it work to her benefit. She discovered that much of her time during the day was devoted to thinking about food. Part of the thinking about food was necessary, as when planning meals, but a lot of it was sheer fantasizing. She learned how to let go of these thoughts by using the training she received in Creative Relaxation. Each time she became aware that she was thinking about food, she would let go of the thought, as she learned from practicing the Personal Quiet Time. As soon as she let go of the thought, she would be more absorbed in what she was doing, or she would find something else to do.

Adequate sleep is another important component of the Basic Four. Many people think that when they are tired, they need to sleep. This may not always be what your body needs. Much of the tiredness we feel is related to physical and emotional fatigue. According to a psychiatrist, Stewart Battle of Mount Sinai Hospital in New York, almost 80 percent of all chronic tiredness is due to emotional fatigue. Misdirecting your stress by worrying about an illness in the family, about making your money stretch to pay the bills, or about arguments with your spouse can waste your adaptive energy. Boredom or suffering from too little stress can be just as tiring. Dealing with emotional fatigue by collapsing into bed is not a good alternative. Getting into bed may only make things worse.

Physical fatigue arises when you have used your muscles too much. It is interesting to note that when one set of muscles is overused, the nearby muscles are affected. That explains why using your arms all day out in the yard on the weekend causes your whole body to feel weary. Sleeping when you are physically tired because of overusing your muscles is not what your body needs.

Many people use sleep as a way to avoid dealing with problems or conflicts. Individuals quickly discover that sleep does not solve their problems. Nevertheless, sleep is important. Much is needed to be learned about the purpose of sleep. It has been found that both humans and animals need to dream. Studies by researchers show that when a person is deprived of dreams he begins to suffer psychological abnormalities and physical symptoms. When we are deprived of the dream state by loss of sleep, by drugs, by anxiety, or by deliberate awakenings, we quickly compensate by making it up with sleep.

You may have days when you wake up more tired than when you went to sleep. If so, you are likely suffering from either emotionally or physically related fatigue. Many people are surprised to learn that even though sleep and relaxation are both hypometabolic states, they are not the same. Some researchers state that relaxation is more restful than sleep. Consider a 220-pound man getting into a neatly made bed for the night. Throughout the night he tosses and turns numerous times, as can be seen by the disorder of the sheets in the morning. Each time he moved throughout the night, his body was activated; his muscles contracted and lengthened, his breathing and heart rate altered, and his blood pressure changed. During relaxation or meditation, however, the metabolism slows down as long as the person continues to relax.

One of the physiological differences between sleep and relaxation is in oxygen consumption. During sleep, oxygen consumption is gradually and progressively reduced; after about four or five hours of sleep it is about 8 percent lower than during wakefulness. Researchers have recorded that during relaxation or meditation there is approximately a 10 to 20 percent decrease in oxygen consumption after only three minutes of practicing a relaxation technique. Therefore, you may reduce your stress more quickly and effectively through Creative Relaxation than by a night's rest.

In addition to the drop in oxygen consumption associated with relaxed feelings, there is a marked decrease in blood lactate, a by-product of skeletal muscle metabolism. The blood lactate level drops rapidly within the first ten minutes of relaxation and remains relatively low. The higher the blood lactate level, the greater the anxiety. This helps to explain the relaxed, calm feelings experienced after practicing a relaxation technique.

Creative Relaxation also corresponds to lowered sympathetic nervous system activity. The heart rate decreases, on the average, about three beats per minute during a relaxation technique. During sleep the heart rate lowers about one or two beats per minute. In addition, the respiration rate, or number of breaths per minute, also lowers. Relaxation or meditation is not a form of sleep, nor can it be used as a substitute for sleep. But many practitioners of Creative Relaxation have found that after investing two fifteen-minute Personal Quiet Time periods, they need one to two hours less sleep.

Just as the body needs sleep, it needs to be exercised. Exercise is important because it stresses the body at the same time it conditions it. A lot of people confuse exercise with relaxation. Exercise is not the same thing as relaxation, yet both of them are good for you. Most people think of playing golf, jogging, or playing tennis as relaxation. Such activities may help make you feel better, but they are not relaxation. Relaxation, as you will recall, is when you are at ease physically, chemically, emotionally, and mentally.

Exercise differs from relaxation in two main ways: the first difference is in the physical state produced. When you play a rough game of tennis or take your daily jog, the parameters of your body are activated. Your heart rate, blood pressure, and breathing rate are elevated in an effort to supply enough oxygen to the muscles. You feel yourself sweating and your muscles contracting and lengthening as you move. Your body is under more stress when you exercise.

Relaxation, on the other hand, has an opposite effect on the body. It lets all of the various organs and systems slow down until the body reaches a hypometabolic state.

Exercise is a mental diversion. It lets you keep your mind off various problems. Exercise helps you to release bottled-up tensions that destroy energy. Some people think that the training from exercise is relaxation because ultimately the heart rate, breathing rate, and blood pressure lower. The effect on your body after training daily in a supervised exercise program is still not relaxation.

Suppose your heart rate was 78 beats per minute before you started the exercise program. When you practice a relaxation technique, your heart rate will lower about three beats per minute, or the heart will beat about 75 times per minute. After six weeks of exercising daily, the person's heart rate drops, let's say, to a resting heart rate of 72 beats per minute. But even though the heart rate lowers, the body will continue to respond differently during relaxation. If your heart rate has been lowered to 72 beats per minute, doing a relaxation technique will lower your heart rate on the average to 69 beats per minute. Relaxation lets the body rest, whereas exercise adds stress to the body.

You exercise and relax for different purposes. The purpose of exercise is to condition the body so that it can recover more quickly and easily from stressful situations. At the same time, exercise refreshes you mentally. It also tones your muscles and increases the efficiency of your heart and circulatory system, thereby making you even more resistant to stress.

Exercising your body can be likened to taking a car out on the racetrack for a trial run. Just as the car is pushed to its maximum level of functioning, so is your body. On the day of the actual race, the driver of the car knows how best to drive that car. Likewise, when you are faced with a stressful situation, your body knows how to adjust to the additional stresses.

If exercise is like a trial run, relaxation is equivalent to a tune-up. Relaxation techniques like Creative Relaxation help to replenish the body after being battered by stress throughout the day.

Researchers are continuing to demonstrate the relationship between stress and disease. When stress is misdirected over a period of time, or when a stress reaction is severe enough, physical harm results. The most common stress-related illnesses include hypertension, ulcers, heart attacks, asthma, hay fever, and migraine headaches. Some researchers are associating such diseases as allergies, arthritis, and cancer with stress.

Dr. Hans Selye contends that illness and disease result when the body's adaptive mechanism falters. The theory of disease and illness is explained by Dr. Selye through the GAS (General Adaptation Syndrome) and the LAS (Local Adaptation Syndrome) mechanisms.

As you will recall, stress is the sum of changes that occur at one time. The GAS, on the other hand, encompasses all the nonspecific changes that occur over a period of time during continued exposure to a stressor. The GAS accounts for the normal wear and tear on the body as one goes through life. This evolution of adaptation, as Dr. Selye refers to it, consists of three stages: the alarm reaction, the stage of resistance, and the stage of exhaustion. At any given moment, you and I are under stress during these stages. In time, certain symptoms can occur and be identified. Most of the demands placed upon us, including infections, physical and mental exertions, and other stressors that act upon us for a limited amount of time, produce changes in the first two stages. Only in the most severe stress, or when all of our adaptive energy is used, will the third stage of general exhaustion and death follow.

We can progress through all three stages without dying when only parts of the body are affected. For example, jogging is a stress-producing situation. At first, the body is alerted and makes numerous changes in order to meet the demands placed upon it. After jogging a certain distance, the body moves easily and efficiently, but eventually exhaustion occurs and the jogger must stop. This can be compared to the stages of alarm, resistance, and exhaustion in the GAS. Since primarily the cardiovascular and muscular systems of the body were taxed for a limited time, the body is able to recover after a short rest. Another example of pure muscle exhaustion is trying to flex your index finger rapidly for several minutes. At first it is easy, but your finger soon tires, until you can no longer flex it. That's the stage of exhaustion.

The selective exhaustion of only specific areas of the body represents the final stages of the LAS. Several LASs may occur simultaneously. The GAS can be activated if the intensity or extent of the LAS is great enough.

Disease and illness set in when there is an imperfection in the GAS mechanism. It is theorized that diseases are not only the result of being exposed to an outside agent such as an infection or intoxication; they are outcomes of the body's inability to adjust to these agents. No malady, however, is strictly a disease of adaption. On the other hand, there are no diseases that can be so perfectly handled by the organism that maladaptation plays no part in their effects upon the body. Dr. Selye's concept of disease supports Louis Pasteur's statement made in the 1800s: "The microbe is nothing, the terrain is everything." This may help to clarify why, when a number of people are exposed to a germ, not all will get ill.

Each of us suffers from illness or disease at one time or another. Creative Relaxation has been found to be helpful in alleviating some of the discomforts of being sick. Practicing the Personal Quiet Time regularly twice a day helps to conserve the body's energy so that it can be used to combat the germ.

Creative Relaxation used in combination with various medications has been found to be helpful in hastening the time of recovery. Many people are effectively using the technique to help reduce pain.

For instance, Alice suffered from a throbbing type of pain. Each time she tried to fight the pain, it got worse. She learned to eliminate the pain while practicing the Personal Quiet Time. Each of the muscles is relaxed as usual. When she reaches the point of pain, she allows it to throb. Rather than fight the pain as before, she latches on to the throbbing sensation. Each time the throbbing occurs, she imagines the area relaxing; at the same time she imagines the pain getting less and less severe. It is as if the pain is like a burning candle, slowly burning itself out. She concentrates on relaxing only about fifteen to twenty seconds and then moves on to relax another muscle group. Toward the end of the relaxation period, she may return to the painful area and go through the process again.

Once she was able to eliminate the pain during the Personal Quiet Time, she learned to benefit from the process during more stressful times in her day. When she felt the pain rising, she would stop what she was doing and concentrate on transferring the relaxed feelings from the Personal Quiet Time, following the same procedure, and relaxing the painful area.

People who suffer from a dull, aching sensation eliminate the pain by following the same process as Alice, except instead of attaching to the pain and imagining the pain getting duller and duller, they visualize the pain "seeping its way out" of the body.

Creative Relaxation is not a cure-all. It is not meant to be a substitute for medical treatment. The technique is designed to be practiced as a complement to one's daily life. It is an integral component of living a quality life, and it is one of the Basic Four—adequate sleep, proper diet, regular exercise, and Creative Relaxation daily.

Appendixes

BRIEF SUMMARY OF THE
CREATIVE RELAXATION TECHNIQUE

Progression I

1. Learn how specifically to tighten muscles.
2. Let thoughts go by returning attention to muscles.

Progression II

1. Learn how to incorporate your own preference for tightening a muscle before relaxing it.
2. Breathe smoothly and regularly.

Purposes of Progressions I and II

1. Learn how maximally to tighten a muscle in the best way for you.
2. Learn how to relax a muscle after maximally tightening it.
3. Recognize when a muscle is tightened and when it is relaxed.

Progression III

1. Learn to breathe with abdominal muscles.
2. Create relaxed feelings in the muscles without tightening them first.
3. Let thoughts go easily by not feeling you have to solve any problems at this time.

Progression IV

1. Decide whether you want to:
   a. use music;
   b. imagine yourself in a scene or not;
   c. tighten all or several muscle groups.
2. Thoughts can be there, but you do not need to "top yourself" at this time.

Purposes of Progressions III and IV

1. Learn how to relax muscles quickly and easily in order to integrate relaxed feelings into your daily activities.
2. Learn to "let go of thoughts" to prevent frustrations from lingering throughout the day.

Progression V (Advanced Progression)

The Personal Quiet Time is a skill. At this stage you should fully understand and be able to practice the other four steps comfortably. Most important, you should be able to relax your muscles easily regardless of whether they were contracted first or not. Technique lasts for ten to twelve minutes. The shortened amount of time is acceptable because you can now reach the relaxed state more quickly.

The steps are:

1. Sit comfortably.
2. Breathe smoothly and deeply.
3. Place yourself in your imaginary scene.
4. Contract all your muscles at once, then relax the entire body as you focus attention on both feet at once. After they feel comfortable, relax the lower and upper portions of each leg.
5. The muscles in the buttocks are easily relaxed as you focus yourself in the scene. The stomach and back muscles are guided into relaxing.
6. Focus on letting thoughts easily come and go.
7. Relax the muscles in the neck and shoulder area. As an aid in relaxing, imagine yourself getting a neck massage.
8. Relax both hands. Allow the sensation to travel to the muscles in the lower and upper portions of each arm.
9. Relax all of the muscles in your face.
10. Remain calm and still and enjoy your scene before going back into activity.

THE IDEAL ENVIRONMENT

The variety of scenes that you can create to help you relax and channel stress more positively is endless. The following is a list of some of the more popular scenes that practitioners of Creative Relaxation have used.

- Winter snow scene in the mountains; lying on a soft rug next to a crackling fire in a cozy log cabin

- Summer beach scene with a spectacular sunset; lying on crystal white sand that has been warmed by the sun's rays
- Fall scene in the mountains; lying under a tree, capturing the aroma and beauty of a forest in autumn
- Sailboat scene; an early-morning sunrise with the sailboat gliding across calm waters
- Spaceship in outer space; enjoying the floating sensation and endless boundaries
- Spring showers in a forest; warming yourself by a campfire, sheltered under an old tin roof
- Nature's splendor in the morning scene; the dew from the night sparkles on the leaves as the sun peers through the leaves; all is calm, the fire still burns from the long night and soothes your body as you cuddle near it for warmth
- Lying on a raft floating aimlessly in a sparkling pool with the sun's rays penetrating your skin as it relaxes your body
- A sea of grass; lying in an open field with tall grass and wildflowers bending and swaying with the breeze
- Evening by the sea; lying on a warm, sandy, secluded beach under a black sky with sparkling stars
- Hot fudge with whipped cream; placing yourself in a huge vat of hot fudge as you nestle in soft mounds of whipped cream
- A warm Roman bath with swirling water; enjoying the sensation of the moving water
- A mountain stream; relaxing alongside a running brook, feeling the warm sunlight soothing your body as you hear the bubbling of the water
- Mounds of shaving cream; the erotic feeling of lying in huge swirls of warm, mentholated lather

- A magic carpet; feeling yourself floating freely as the carpet guides you through space
- A glider in the sky; gliding freely and silently across the open sky
- Lakeside solitude; lying on a soft blanket underneath a huge tree that overlooks a lake with still waters
- Moving waters; lying in a shallow, sparkling stream; feeling water flow along your body as the warmth of the sun radiates through the leaves of the trees
- Waterbed delight; lying on a luxurious waterbed, feeling beams of sunlight radiating on your face from the sunroof overhead

Favorite Times and Places

Suggested opportune times and places to practice the Personal Quiet Time of Creative Relaxation:
- As a passenger in a car
- When traveling on an airplane, train, or bus
- In the office:
    during an afternoon break
    before lunch
    before leaving the office
- After arriving home from a day's work
- In the morning after waking up
- Before falling asleep at night
- In your car at a quiet spot on the side of the road before going home
- Before an important event, such as an exam, a presentation, a competitive meet, or a court hearing

Music to Relax by

Let your personal taste guide your selection from the following suggestions:

Easy Listening Artists
  Herb Alpert (trumpet)
  Burt Bacharach (orchestra)
  Percy Faith (orchestra)
  Ferrante and Teicher (pianos)
  Arthur Fiedler and the Boston Pops (orchestra)
  André Kostelanetz (orchestra)
  Los Indios Tabajaras (guitars)
  Michel Legrand (orchestra)
  Henry Mancini (orchestra)
  Mantovani (orchestra)
  Hugo Montenegro (orchestra)
  Mystic Moods (orchestra)
  Peter Nero (piano)
  101 Strings (orchestra)
  Roger Williams (piano)

Movie Soundtracks
  Butch Cassidy and the Sundance Kid
  Doctor Zhivago
  Gone with the Wind
  Ice Castles
  Love Story
  A Man and a Woman
  Midnight Cowboy
  Oliver's Story
  Romeo and Juliet
  Star Wars
  Summer of '42
  A Summer Place
  The Thomas Crown Affair
  The Umbrellas of Cherbourg

Watership Down
The Way We Were

Classical Composers and Recommended Works

Beethoven ("Moonlight" Sonata)
Brahms (Symphony no. 3, third movement; "Lullaby")
Aaron Copland (Appalachian Spring)
Debussy (Prelude to The Afternoon of a Faun, "Claire de Lune")
Haydn (chamber music)
Smetana (Die Moldau)
Johann Strauss ("The Blue Danube" and other waltzes)
Tchaikovsky (Romeo and Juliet overture, Swan Lake, Nutcracker, Sleeping Beauty)
Vivaldi (The Four Seasons)
Wagner (Prelude to Tristan und Isolde)

Classical Artists

Julian Bream (guitar)
Vladimir Horowitz (piano)
Andrés Segovia (guitar)
John Williams (guitar)
Narciso Yepes (guitar)

Jazz Artists

Count Basie
Miles Davis
Duke Ellington
Stan Getz
Bob James
Keith Jarrett
Tim Weisberg

Pop Artists

Leo Kotke (guitar)
Pentangle (assorted combinations)
John Renbourn (guitar)
Tim Weisberg (flute)
Paul Winter Consort (assorted combinations)

Country Artists

Chet Atkins (guitar)
Floyd Cramer (piano)
Charlie McCoy (harmonica)

Songs from All Categories

"Alfie"
"Almost like Being in Love" (from *Hello Dolly*)
"Bali Hai" (from *South Pacific*)
"Bridge over Troubled Waters"
"By the Time I Get to Phoenix"
"California Dreams"
"Don't Let the Sun Catch You Crying"
"Ebb Tide"
"Ferry 'cross the Mersey"
"For the Good Times"
"Help Me Make It through the Night"
"I Don't Know How to Love Him" (from *Jesus Christ Superstar*)
"The Look of Love"
"Maria" (from *West Side Story*)
"Misty"
"Moon River"
"My Way"
"Nadia's Theme"

"Never My Love"
"Norwegian Wood"
"On the Street Where You Live" (from *My Fair Lady*)
"People Will Say We're in Love"
"San Francisco"
"Scarborough Fair"
"Send In the Clowns" (from *A Little Night Music*)
"Smile"
"Summertime" (from *Porgy and Bess*)
"Sunny"
"Sunrise, Sunset" (from *Fiddler on the Roof*)
"(They Long to Be) Close to You"
"Trains and Boats and Planes"
"Unchained Melody"
"A Whiter Shade of Pale"
"Windmills of Your Mind"
"Yesterday"
"You Don't Bring Me Flowers"
"You'll Never Walk Alone" (from *Carousel*)